LEAD WITH INTENT BY ARNE PEDERSEN

Cover Design by **pulse creative partners** (pulsecreativepartners.com)
Interior Design by **IBJ Custom Publishing** (ibjcustompublishing.com)

ISBN 978-0-9776675-6-7
© 2007

INTRODUCTION

There are many, many definitions of what leadership in the marketplace is today. A variety of speakers from various backgrounds have written books, published articles, and spoken at many events. Even with all of this information, the question has remained unanswered. Indeed, what is leadership? Many of you who are reading this book, candidly, have attended these events, read the books and articles, and have planned to use one nugget or two with your employees at your workplace. More times than not, it did not go as planned and thus was chalked up to experience and the materials began to collect dust on shelf space at work or at home. Still, you are left pondering, what is leadership and how do I exemplify this in my company to help us break through and grow? We will discover this together in Part 1 of this book.

There is no easy answer, to be sure. You will not find it in a McDonald's drive thru or in a periodical in the library. In other words, leadership is not fast and easy. In stark contrast, it is a hard, daily life.

With the retiring of the baby-boomers and the emergence of both Generations X and Y, a leadership gap has evolved. Are either of these generations prepared to take the mantle of leadership? What examples do they have? Certainly, we have seen the now famous examples set by Jack Welch (Good) and Jeff Skilling (Bad). Has there been enough investment, training, and nurturing of leaders? Indeed, time will tell. But still the question remains for these generations. Do they know what leadership is?

Before we examine the definition of what leadership is, let's discuss some hard truths. Ten percent of the people on planet earth at any given time in history are born leaders. They have been given, or blessed with, leadership qualities. For these few people, taking on a leadership role is second nature. They don't work hard at leading. What about the remaining 90%? It's simple – those who weren't "born" with the gift and are in leadership roles must learn and work at leadership skills daily. The problem is that very few do, and that leads to great dissatisfaction among tremendously skilled, knowledgeable, and talented workers.

A leader does not have to create the strategy, know everything, and do everything. The bottom line is the leader influences people to accomplish objectives through the use of his leadership attributes (beliefs, values, ethics, character, knowledge, and skill). A great example of this is George Washington: a founding father, our first president, and a landowner. His ability to influence people to win our independence through his leadership attributes was incredible. Another great example is Jack Welch, the former CEO and Chairman of General Electric. His ability to influence people to accomplish great achievements through his leadership attributes is still felt today through the men and women who learned under his tutelage and have gone on to successfully start up companies or run existing ones.

Does that mean that a one-time great speech is going to motivate a sales force to grow revenues while maintaining a reasonable industry standard cost of sales? Not really. It takes a lot of work to influence each of us to make a decision to follow someone. In other words, it does not occur overnight. It takes time for people to trust the leader. The leader takes the greatest risk in putting forth trust unaware of who will return that trust.

The future leaders of our society, whether they are business, political, or community leaders, each one must have an investment in learning and developing leadership, training in leadership, a nurturing environment to further develop leadership, and the discipline to execute leadership daily. As with any investment, some type of measurement must be applied to ensure value has been received. In the case of leadership, the employee economic value added is the correct measurement. In this book, we will refer to this as "leadership measurement." Leadership measurement is derived from the economic profit measurement which includes return on investment, cost of capital, and invested capital. The new measurement takes into account employee productivity and costs.

Furthermore, the leadership measurement needs tests to be relevant. We do this to better measure and understand the success or failure of leadership. In this book, we will focus on three tests for the leadership measurement. The tests are for a positive slope, positive values, and consistency. To demonstrate how this works, part 2 of this book has five different case studies.

Please join me in studying, examining, learning, and understanding leadership and its application in the marketplace.

PART 1:
WHAT IS LEADERSHIP?

"A Commander will command."
GENERAL GEORGE S. PATTON, JR.

CONCEPT OF LEADERSHIP

"The price of greatness is responsibility."
WINSTON CHURCHILL

DEFINITION

Leadership is a process by which a person influences others to accomplish objectives.

A person carries out this process by applying his leadership attributes (beliefs, values, ethics, character, knowledge, and skills). When an employee is deciding if they will respect you, they do not think about each of these attributes of a leader. They watch what you _do_ so that they can tell what you really _are_. They sense if you are an honorable leader or a self-serving phony who misuses his authority to look good and receive promotions and accolades.

PHILOSOPHY

To begin any discussion on leadership, we need to come to grips with learning and describing the philosophy of leadership. The American Heritage Dictionary states that a philosophy is a system of values by which one lives. As applied to leadership, this philosophy changes to reflect a system of values by which one *leads*.

For example, my personal leadership philosophy is the HIL concept. It stands for honesty, integrity, and loyalty. Each word has a different meaning. Honesty means to always tell the truth, even when it hurts. Integrity means to always do what you say you are going to do, even when you don't want to. Loyalty means a two-way trust between people. As a leader, you must make yourself vulnerable by giving loyalty first without regard for return loyalty.

What I have found is that by living this philosophy and thoroughly explaining it to my employees, both in the Army and in corporate America, my employees were honest, demonstrated integrity, were loyal, worked hard, and grew professionally and personally.

PRINCIPLES

The second subject to cover before beginning any discussion on leadership is the "principles of leadership." These are general principles and they apply to every leader irrespective of where they serve. An important note on these principles is that your employees judge you daily on these very principles and do so subconsciously. If you report to another leader, you do the same to him.

Learn these principles and then consciously apply them and watch the transformation, not only of yourself, but of your team as well.

Know Yourself and Seek Self-improvement

As a leader, you need to know who you are including your strengths and weaknesses. Additionally, you need to seek self-improvement. Don't frustrate yourself or your employees; leaders must focus their self-improvement on further improving their strengths and how to better manage their weaknesses. If you don't know yourself and seek self-improvement, you will not garner the respect needed as a leader from anyone.

Be Technically and Tactically Proficient

As a leader, you must know your job. Knowing your job includes knowing the industry and market segment that your company is in. It means knowing the products and services that your company sells. It means knowing and understanding business well enough to enable you to make reasonably intelligent decisions. Also, you need to understand the company, market segment, and industry politics and how to work and live in these environments.

I want to make it painfully clear that you, as a leader, are not supposed to be the expert. Individual contributors are the experts. That's what they do and they enjoy it. They need leaders who know the subject and can have an intelligent conversation. If you don't know enough about it, have them teach you. You will be amazed at the connection you make and the respect you earn.

Seek Responsibility and Take Responsibility for Your Actions

In order to grow as a leader, you need to continue to seek more or different responsibilities. This will help you to grow and stretch both personally and professionally. Leaders want responsibility.

Leaders always take responsibility for their actions and those of their employees. This requires understanding loyalty, which is undergirded by beliefs, values, and norms.

Make Sound and Timely Decisions

Leaders make decisions every day. Those decisions must be sound. Therefore, leaders need a model by which to make decisions. This helps to be disciplined in gathering information, analyzing it, charting prospective courses of action, and making the final decision. We will learn more about this in a later chapter.

Timely decision-making is important as well. It can help avoid costly mistakes in human capital, capital, other tangible and intangible resources, and

14

time. It can launch or sink a company. Leaders must understand timing in all their decisions.

Set the Example

As a leader, you have expectations of your employees. You communicate them both verbally and non-verbally. The communication style that is most effective is non-verbal. If you expect your employees to do something, you had better do it as well. If you don't, you'll be thought of as a phony.

Know Your Employees

As a leader, you must know your employees. They are people with skills, knowledge, experience, families, emotions, etc. They come from diverse backgrounds and communicate in a variety of frames. They are at various levels of maturity both personally and professionally. You must connect with your people in order to know them.

As a leader, you must also look out for the well-being of your employees. They are demanding and trusting you to do so. The ultimate outcome is a stronger and better team.

Keep Your Employees Informed

As a leader, you need to trust your employees with the information needed to do their jobs and to keep them focused. Unless you are bound by confidentiality or timing constraints, keep your employees informed. In the absence of information, people will make it up from their own frame of mind. This promotes anarchy and reduces the effectiveness of leadership.

Develop a Sense of Responsibility for Your Employees

As a leader, you must look at your employees as your responsibility. During the time of their employ under your leadership, you have the responsibility to help advance them in their career. You read that correctly! You own the responsibility! Keep in mind the balance of the employee having responsibility to act on the opportunities and the coaching you provide.

Ensure that the Task is Understood, Supervised, and Accomplished

As a leader, your most important job is to communicate, communicate, and communicate. This is said three times not because you need to say the same message three times. Rather, you must understand the frame from which each employee learns and communicates, and communicate the message in a relevant way to them.

Once they have received the message, you need to remove hurdles for them, keep them accountable, and celebrate successful accomplishments with them. It's a great opportunity to connect and grow in your relationships with your employees.

Train and Inspire Your Employees as a Team

As a leader, you have people reporting to you. While these are individuals, they must also learn to work together as a team. Developing and implementing training for them as a team will help build the necessary *espirit de corps* you need to lead your team.

When your employees work together as a team, they solve problems together as a team, build businesses together as a team, and grow personally and professionally as a team. This leadership nirvana will enable you to focus on strategic planning.

Deploy Your Employees in Accordance with Their Capabilities

As a leader, you need to know your employees' strengths and weaknesses and how they fit together on your team. Trying to force people into roles that don't play to their strengths and the strengths of the team will result in frustration for all parties and you will lose people. Putting them in the roles that play to their strengths as individuals and as a team will promote the harmony, goodwill, and discipline of the team. Your employees will have the opportunity to learn and grow in a positive environment.

FACTORS

The four factors of leadership are the follower, the leader, communication, and the situation.

The Follower

The first major factor of leadership is the follower. Different employees require different styles of leadership. A young or new employee may require more direct supervision than that of an older or more experienced employee. An employee with a poor attitude requires a different approach than a highly motivated employee. You must know your employees if you want to take the right leadership actions at the right time.

The fundamental starting point for knowing your employees is a clear understanding of human nature (needs, emotions, and motivation). You also need the trust, respect, and confidence of key people other than your employees. You need the willing assistance of certain peers, key support personnel, and your superior. You need to understand the _be_, _know_, and _do_[1] attributes of these key people. You must behave in a manner which motivates them to want to help you. This can only happen when you have developed relationships of mutual trust, respect, and confidence with them.

Finally, you are a follower as well as a leader. You have to find ways to meet the needs and goals of your superiors, your employees, other key people, and yourself. To accomplish this, you need to do the same thing. You must understand key people, have good communication with them, and develop relationships based on trust and respect.

The Leader

The second major factor of leadership is you – the leader. You must have an honest understanding of who you are, what you know, and what you can do. This is necessary in order for you to control and discipline yourself and to lead your employees effectively.

---

[1] Adapted from FM 22-100 Military Leadership, October 1983, p. 49, Leadership Framework

Before we go any further, you need to honestly explore and understand who you are, what you know, and what you can do. Please take 30 minutes to answer the following questions:

PRACTICAL EXERCISE:

I. Who are you?

_____

_____

_____

_____

_____

II. What do you know?

_____

_____

_____

_____

_____

III. What can you do?

_____

_____

_____

_____

_____

Now that you've answered these very important questions, you are ready to move on to the next factor of leadership: Communication.

Communication

The third major factor of leadership is communication. You lead through two-way communication. Much of this is nonverbal. When you "set the example," for instance, that communicates to your employees that you will share hardship with them and will not ask them to do anything you are not willing to do. Leadership is more than setting the example and bravely leading a charge.

You teach, coach, counsel, persuade, and punish through verbal and nonverbal communication.

The way you communicate in various situations is important. Your choice of words, tone of voice, body language, and the look in your eye affect the way an employee *feels* about what you communicate.

The right word – spoken quietly at the right moment – is also an important part of leadership.

What and how you communicate either builds or harms the strength of the relationship between you and your employees.

In a healthy relationship between people, there are bonds of mutual trust, respect, confidence, and understanding. These bonds form the basis for discipline and cohesion in the organization. They are built over time as your employees learn – from training, from working together, from experience, and from what you communicate – that you are a competent leader whom they can trust and respect.

The Situation

The fourth major factor of leadership is the situation. Let's be clear… **all situations are different**. Leadership that worked in one situation with one group of employees, superiors, and other key people may not work in another situation. Many forces combine to determine the best leadership action to take at a particular time. Also, by identifying and influencing certain forces, you can create a situation more favorable to plan execution.

There are no rules or formulas to tell you exactly what to do. You need to understand principles of leadership, tactics, and human nature and to apply these as guides in particular situations. Then use your judgment to decide the best action to take and which leadership style to use.

The leadership situation includes all the forces affecting your business and the well-being of your employees. Examples of forces are your relationship with your superiors, the skill of your employees, the organization of your department/team, and the informal leaders in the department/team. There are a plethora of forces. No list is complete.

The situation includes all the forces that affect the ability and motivation of your organization to accomplish its objectives. You must be skilled in identifying and thinking through the important forces in a situation. Then you will be able to take the right action at the right time.

What if you take the wrong action? It happens. We all make mistakes. Analyze the situation again, take quick corrective action, and move on to the next challenge. *Learn from your mistakes and those of others.*

LEADERSHIP STYLES

Leadership style is the personal manner and approach of leading (providing purpose, direction, and motivation). It is the way leaders directly interact with their employees. Effective leaders are flexible in the way they interact with employees. They deal with employees differently, changing the way they interact as an employee develops or as the situation changes. Your manner and approach of leading will obviously depend on your training, education, experience, and view of the world. You have to be yourself, yet flexible enough to adjust to the people you lead and to the plans you are executing.

Some say they admire a certain leader because he always seems to know exactly what to do in a particular situation, or they admire a leader who knows just the right words to say at the right time to ensure the objectives are met and employees are cared for. Experience has taught you that you should not deal with all people in the same manner. For example, you know it is not effective to deal with a new employee the same as you would deal with an experienced manager or individual contributor.

For years, when people talked about leadership styles, they thought about two extremes – an autocratic style and a democratic style. Autocratic leaders used their legitimate authority and the power of their position to get results while democratic leaders used their personality to persuade and involve employees in solving problems and making decisions. Consideration of these two options alone limit the possibility of a leader using different styles and being flexible enough to be autocratic at times and democratic at other times, or to combine the two extreme styles at still other times.

There are three basic styles of leadership…directing, participating, and delegating.

Directing

A leader is using the directing leadership style when he tells employees what he wants done, how he wants it done, where he wants it done, when he wants it done, and then supervises closely to ensure they follow his directions. This style is clearly appropriate in many situations. When time is short and you alone know what needs to be done and how to do it, this style is the best way to execute a plan.

When leading employees who lack experience or competence at a task, you need to direct their behavior using this style. They will not resent your close supervision. You will be giving them what they need and want. In fact, asking inexperienced employees to help you solve complex problems or plan an operation would be frustrating for them.

If a leader announces that the team will be developing a market analysis using the five forces model and the SWOT analysis and looking at specific competitors, he is using the directing style of leadership. He did not ask for any information or recommendations before making and announcing his decision.

Some people think that a leader is using the directing style when he yells, uses demeaning language, or threatens and intimidates employees. This is **not** the directing style. It is simply an ***abusive***, ***unprofessional*** way to treat employees.

Participating

A leader is using the participating leadership style when he involves employees in determining what to do and how to do it. The leader asks for information and recommendations, however, he still makes the decisions. He simply gets advice from employees before making the decision. This style is appropriate for many leadership situations.

If your employees have some competence and support your goals, allowing them to participate can be a powerful team-building process. It will build their confidence and increase their support for the final plan if they help develop it. If a leader asks employees to recommend various approaches, tools, and companies to review before making his final plans, he is using the participating style of leadership. He still makes the decision but considers information and recommendations from his employees first.

Do not be concerned that asking an employee for advice or using an employee's good plan or idea shows weakness. The opposite is true; it is a sign of strength that your employees will respect. On the other hand, you are responsible for the quality of your plans and decisions. If you believe an idea one of your employees offers is not a good one, you must reject the idea and do what you believe is right, regardless of pressure to do otherwise.

Delegating

A leader is using the delegating leadership style when he delegates problem-solving and decision-making authority to an employee or to a group of employees. This style is appropriate when dealing with mature employees who support your goals and are competent and motivated to perform the task delegated. While you are always accountable to your superior for the results of any task you delegate, you must hold your employees accountable to you for their actions and performance.

If a leader tasks an experienced and motivated employee to lead a market analysis project, he is using the delegating style of leadership. Some things are appropriate to delegate, others are not. The key is to release your employees' problem-solving potential while you determine what problems they should solve and help them learn to solve them.

Choosing a Leadership Style

Choosing the correct style of leadership requires you to understand the four factors of leadership that we covered earlier. You, the leader, must size up every situation and employee carefully to choose the right style. Consider how competent, motivated, and committed those you lead are to handle the situation at hand. Have they done it before? Were they successful? Will they need your supervision, direction, or encouragement?

The answers to these questions will help you choose the best leadership style and manner to communicate so that your employees will understand your intent and want to help you execute a plan. As a leader you want to develop and train your employees so that you can confidently delegate tasks to them. The delegating style is the most efficient of the three leadership styles. It requires the least amount of your time and energy to interact, direct, and communicate with your employees. Because it is the most efficient style, it is in your best interest to use the delegating style with as many of your employees and as much of the time as possible.

But before you can use the delegating leadership style, you must train and develop your employees. An inexperienced employee needs your direction. You must tell him what needs to be done and how to do it. After he gains some competence, and if he is motivated and shares your goals, you can reduce the amount of supervision you give to him. Encourage him, ask him for advice, and allow him to participate in helping you make plans and decisions. With time, experience, and your skillful leadership, this person will gain even more competence and become even more motivated and committed to helping the team accomplish its objectives. When you have trained and developed an employee to this level of competence and commitment, use the delegating style of leadership. As situations change or as new goals or objectives are assigned, you will need to continue to be flexible in the leadership style you use. Even though you have successfully used the delegating leadership style with an employee, you may need to temporarily return to the directing style of leadership if you give him an unfamiliar or new task. Because the employee is unfamiliar with the task, you will need to tell him what to do and how to do it.

As the employee gains competence, confidence, and motivation in this new task, you can gradually shift your style again to the participating or delegating style. By assessing the leadership needs of your employees, you can determine what leadership style to use. Do not confuse emotion with styles of leadership!

Finally, there is no one best leadership style. What works in one situation may not work in another. You must develop the flexibility to use all three styles. Furthermore, you must develop the judgment to choose the style that best meets the situation and the needs of the employee.

ATTRIBUTES

If you are a leader, your employees can trust you to accomplish the objectives while looking out for their well-being, and you will earn their respect!

To be a competent leader there are certain things that you must *be*, *know*, and *do*. Below, you will see the be, know, and do Leadership Framework. This is an encompassing approach to leadership. We cover these topics in more depth later in the book. I wanted to expose you to the framework now so that you can see how the successive chapters and their respective content fit into leadership.

LEADERSHIP FRAMEWORK

AS A LEADER YOU MUST		EXAMPLES
BE	Be commited to ethical professionalism	Loyalty to the company's vision and mission, loyalty to your department, selfless service, and personal responsibility
	Possess professional character traits	Courage, competance, candor, commitment, and integrity
KNOW	Know the four factors of leadership and how they affect each other	Follower, leader, communication, and situation
	Know yourself	Strengths and weakness of your character, knowledge, and skill
	Know human nature	• Human needs and emotions • How people respond to stress • Strengths and weakness of the character, knowledge, and skills of your empolyees
	Know your job	Technical and tactical proficiency
	Know your department/team	• How to develop necessary individual and team skills • How to develop cohesion • How to develop discipline
DO	Provide direction	Goal setting, problem solving, decision making, and planning
	Implement	Communicating, coordinating, supervision, and evaluating
	Motivate	Applying principles of motivation such as developing morale and espirit in your department/team; teaching, coaching, and counseling

Adapted from FM 22-100 Military Leadership, October 1983, p. 49, Leadership Framework

PRACTICAL EXERCISE

I. Identify someone you know who characterizes leadership.

A. How does this person influence others?

_____

_____

_____

B. Describes this person's leadership attributes.

_____

_____

_____

II. What are the four factors of leadership? What does each factor mean to you? How does the person identified above model these factors?

_____

_____

_____

III. A leader must ___, ____, and ____ to be effective.

IV. Given the information in this section, how will you model your behavior for leadership in the future?

_____

_____

SUMMARY

In this chapter, we have defined leadership as the process by which a person influences others to accomplish objectives. He carries out this process by applying his leadership attributes (beliefs, values, ethics, character, knowledge, and skills).

We've gone through the factors of leadership (the follower, the leader, communication, and the situation), and briefly outlined what a leader must *be*, *know*, and *do* to be effective.

Taken together, the definition, the factors, and the required *be*, *know* and *do* leadership attributes provide a philosophy or concept of professional leadership that will help you develop yourself, your employees, and your team. It will also help you address the challenges that every leader faces.

BELIEFS, VALUES, NORMS, AND ETHICS

"The time is always right
to do what is right."

MARTIN LUTHER KING, JR.

BELIEFS, VALUES, AND NORMS

Beliefs

Beliefs are assumptions or convictions that you hold to be true regarding people, concepts, or things. We all have beliefs about people, concepts, and things. One employee may believe that his obligation to his career simply means putting in time from "8 to 5." Another may believe that obligation is selflessly serving the company and customers. We have beliefs about human nature – what makes people tick. We usually cannot prove our beliefs scientifically, but we think and feel that they are true.

Values

Values are attitudes about the worth or importance of people, concepts, or things. You may place high value on a family heirloom, such as your grandfather's watch, or on a clean, well-maintained car. You may value personal comfort or freedom to travel. You may value a friend, a relative, or an adult who helped you as you were growing up.

Norms

Norms are standards that govern behavior, and fall into two categories:

Formal – Official standards or laws that govern behavior. Traffic lights, the United States Constitution, agreements or contracts with customers all are formal norms that direct behavior. They dictate what actions are required or forbidden. Safety regulations and codes, and company operating procedures, are also formal norms.

Informal – Unwritten rules or standards that govern the behavior of group members. For example, the U.S. Army has an informal norm that the wounded are evacuated after a battle, regardless of danger. At the root of this norm is a shared value about the importance of caring for each other. Each member of the Army found comfort in knowing that he would be cared for.

PRACTICAL EXERCISE:

I. **What are your beliefs?**

_____

_____

_____

_____

_____

_____

_____

_____

II. **What are your values?**

_____

_____

_____

_____

_____

_____

_____

III. **What norms do you subscribe to?**

_____

_____

_____

_____

Importance of Beliefs, Values, and Norms

Beliefs, values, and norms guide the actions of individuals and groups. They are like a traffic control system; they are signals giving direction, meaning, and purpose to our lives.

They are powerful!

People will risk danger and often die for deeply held beliefs and values. Many early Christians died for their beliefs because they valued service to God more than their lives. Death in the service of God was an accepted norm. Beliefs and values are fundamental motivating factors; leaders should nurture and shape these factors in their employees.

Your employees will support you if they believe that the best chance for success for themselves and their co-workers is to execute their role as part of the team. They will be more effective if they believe in themselves, in the company, in you, and in the purpose of the objectives.

Development

As a leader, you have the power to influence the beliefs and values of your employees by setting an example, rewarding behavior that supports professional beliefs, values, and norms and planning and conducting challenging and realistic individual and team training. For example, ongoing professional training in a specific area, function, or skill, including continuing education (CE), seminars, formal education, will develop empolyees as individuals and team members.

Computer-generated simulations, such as challenging a team in a new market environment, are great examples of team training. You, the leader, are ultimately responsible to provide the access to and promote the participation in training, both individual and team. Be creative in finding great opportunities to improve and unite your employees!

Remember, you can influence beliefs and values in your employees by what you are and what you do. As the leader, you must respect your employees and have their respect if you are to influence their beliefs and values.

Respect is basic to all human relationships. Strong friendships, strong marriages, and strong teams are based on respect. If there is mutual respect between you and your employees, they will be motivated to follow you anywhere!

Influence

As a leader, you should use your influence to promote cohesion and discipline. You do this when you show sincere concern for all employees, both leaders and followers. By being concerned with the personal and professional values, needs, and goals of your employees, and by being deeply involved in the business, you will sense who the informal leaders are.

Gain and maintain the respect of both your formal and informal leaders. Then they will adopt your beliefs, values, concepts, and methods and convince others to do the same.

Remain firm when you sincerely believe you are right, even if it means everyone is temporarily angry with you.

In the long run, if you are right, they will know it and respect your courage.

Admit to all concerned that you were wrong if you did something you believed to be right at the time and circumstances later proved you wrong. This takes humility and moral courage, but you will gain respect.

Some people think it is a sign of weakness to apologize, that a leader loses power if he does.

That is not true! It shows strong character. We are all human, we all make mistakes.

You will find that the simple act of acknowledging your error to the individuals involved makes a big difference when it comes time for that employee to stand up for you.

PRACTICAL EXERCISE:

I. What would your employees say
about your influence?

_____

_____

_____

_____

II. What would your peers say?

_____

_____

_____

_____

III. What do you say?

_____

_____

_____

_____

IV. Have you ever apologized to an employee
when you were wrong? If so, what did it feel
like and what was the ultimate outcome?

_____

_____

PROFESSIONAL VALUES AND ETHICS

The basic professional beliefs and values that you should hold and constantly strive to instill in your formal leaders and employees are loyalty to the ideals of the profession, loyalty to the company, personal responsibility, and selfless service. These four values make up the professional ethic and they should be the basic values of all employees. Irrespective of your management or supervisory position, if you do not live up to these values under pressure, you are not yet a professional leader.

Loyalty to the Ideals of the Profession

The fundamental value of the professional ethic is loyalty to the ideals of the profession. This value implies recognition that the profession exists solely to serve people. It represents an unswerving loyalty to the ideals of the profession, to the people they serve, and to colleagues.

Loyalty to the Company

The second value of the professional ethic implies a two-way obligation between those who lead and those who are led:

- An obligation to enhance lives
- To be considerate of the well-being of one's employees
- To instill a sense of devotion and pride in the company
- To develop the cohesiveness and loyalty that mold individuals into high performance teams

Personal Responsibility

This responsibility includes the age-old values of *duty* and *honor*. As a professional, your responsibility is to do your *duty*, what ought to be done, in an honorable way. The honorable way accords with the moral values of truth and justice. You have *honor* if you morally and courageously do your duty to the best of your ability.

Selfless Service

Service in any company in any role requires teamwork which emphasizes the greater good. Selfless service means putting the needs and goals of others ahead of your personal needs and interests. As a leader, you must be the greatest "servant" in your company. You are not given authority, status, and position as a personal reward to enjoy in comfort. You are given them so that you may be of greater service to your employees, your company, and all shareholders.

A successful leader should be perceived as the hardest-working member of the organization. That does not imply that he does the same work as his employees. He does work appropriate to his position and thereby assists his employees in getting each job done.

PRACTICAL EXERCISE:

I. Where do your loyalties lie?

_____

_____

_____

_____

II. How do you fit the definition of selfless servant?

I do whatever it takes to do the things that need done.

_____

_____

III. What would your employees, peers, and superiors say about you?

I do more than required

_____

_____

_____

Four Professional Values

Courage, candor, competence, and *commitment* are four qualities or traits of character which must be valued by all professionals. They should be the foundation of your character. The more you build these traits in yourself and others, the more successful you will be. In order for them to become traits, you must first believe in and value them.

COURAGE

Courage comes in two forms: physical courage and moral courage. Physical courage is overcoming fears of bodily harm and doing your duty. Moral courage is overcoming fears of other than bodily harm while doing what ought to be done. It is the courage to stand firm on your values or moral principles, knowing that the action may not be in your best interest.

There will be times when honestly stating your true beliefs to your superiors or the group may not be in your best interest – it may hurt your chances for promotion or even ruin your whole career. These times will test whether or not you have the moral courage to "stand up and be counted."

CANDOR

Candor is being frank, open, honest, and sincere with your employees, superiors, peers, and customers. It is an expression of personal integrity.

COMPETENCE

Competence is proficiency in required professional knowledge, judgment, and skills. Each leader must have it to coach, teach, and mentor others and to develop a cohesive and disciplined team to successfully meet stated objectives.

COMMITMENT

Commitment means the dedication to carry out all assigned work and serve the values of your profession and your company, all the while meeting agreed upon objectives.

Definition

A *dilemma* is a situation presenting two or more undesirable alternatives. You face a simple dilemma when you choose between going hungry or eating something you really dislike. An ethical dilemma occurs when two or more values conflict or collide. When you find yourself in an ethical dilemma, you must search for the morally *right* thing to do. The right thing to do is the moral action that best serves the ideals of the company and of your employees. The "highest moral good" is what professional ethics are all about.

Here is a word of advice to you, the leader. If you make the right decisions when faced with ethical problems, you will continually build your character and your leadership.

If you fall into the trap of taking the easy way occasionally, *you will tend to justify your actions and then begin to erode your character.* People will sense this over a period of time and gradually lose respect for you. You will then be forced to use coercion to motivate them and will eventually lose the necessary foundation for positive, inspired leadership.

Pressures to be Unethical

A principle, a belief, or a value is but a concept until it is tested under stress. Anyone can be ethical when there is no pressure to be unethical. If you are a professional, you will resist all pressures to be unethical. Such temptation can come from many directions. It can come from within you, from peers, from employees, or from superiors.

Pressure from Self-Interest

Self-interest is probably the most common cause of unethical acts. An individual does something to improve his personal situation or to avoid criticism or punishment.

What are some examples of pressure from self-interest?

_____

_____

_____

Pressure from a Peer

A peer can also put pressure on you to behave unethically. A peer may ask you to "forget" that you saw him physically or verbally abuse one of his employees or to falsify documents. These acts are breaches of professional ethics because they involve misrepresenting the truth. They contribute to an unethical climate in that they condone and encourage the unethical behavior of others.

What are examples of this?

_____

_____

_____

_____

Pressure from Employees

An employee may approach you about not doing everything you committed to so that the team may do less work without anyone knowing.

What other examples can you think of where an employee applies pressure?

_____

_____

_____

_____

Pressure from a Superior

Pressure to be unethical can come from superiors and their desire to "look good" on audits, statistics, and activities that are visible to their superiors. Your superior can pressure you to do things with the direct or implied threat of an adverse annual review. He might say "I don't care how you do it, but get those deliverables complete in the next five days." Or, he might tell you to collect at least a certain amount for a charitable fund drive. Even if your superior is a supportive, positive type of leader, he represents the leadership of the organization, and thus the chain of command. This in itself can cause indirect pressure upon you to behave unethically.

AN ETHICAL DECISION-MAKING PROCESS

Background

Regardless of the source of the pressure to act unethically, you usually know in your heart the right thing to do. The real question is whether or not you have the character to live by professional values when under pressure. If you have the values we've discussed in this section, the right thing to do in most situations will normally be clear, and you will do it.

You will sometimes find yourself in complex situations where the ethical alternative is not clear. These are the ethical dilemmas where two or more deeply held values collide. In such situations you need a reasoning process to assist you in deciding what course of action results in the greater moral good.

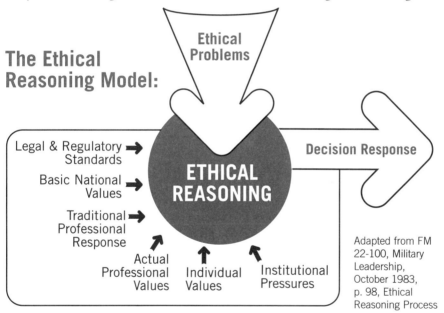

The Ethical Reasoning Model:

Ethical Problems

Legal & Regulatory Standards →

Basic National Values →

Traditional Professional Response →

ETHICAL REASONING

Decision Response

Actual Professional Values

Individual Values

Institutional Pressures

Adapted from FM 22-100, Military Leadership, October 1983, p. 98, Ethical Reasoning Process

Ethical Reasoning Model

When using this model, the ethical problems are introduced into the environment and you, as the leader, now must use ethical reasoning to form a "decision response." As you can see in the illustration, there are a variety of gating factors[2] ranging from values to standards to pressures which are all competing for your "decision response."

---

2 Adapted from FM 22-100, Military Leadership, October 1983, pps. 98 and 99, Ethical Reasoning Process

Let's examine each of these gating factors.

Legal Standards – Formal regulatory standards contained in law.

Basic National Values – Values established in the Constitution, Declaration of Independence, and other documents and traditions that provide the foundation for required behavior of all Americans.

Traditional Professional Values – Values established as standards of required behavior by and for all professionals. They are loyalty to the profession, loyalty to the company, personal responsibility, selfless service, courage, competence, candor, and commitment.

Actual Professional Values – Values actually functioning in companies and the profession that produce the standards governing day-to-day professional behavior. Traditional and actual values usually align. When they don't, there usually is an ethical dilemma.

Individual Values – Values held by the individual professionals involved in the situation.

Institutional Pressures – Elements of various policies, procedures, operations, and other aspects which influence the ethical behavior of professionals.

Complex Ethical Dilemmas

It may seem to you that the ethical reasoning process is too mechanical. You may think you do not need it if you have the will and moral courage to be honest. For most situations, this is true.

However, there are complex ethical dilemmas that need a reasoning model to assist in decision-making. For if you ever decide to violate a policy, procedure, process, regulation, or law, you must be able to show that your actions were not motivated by self-gain but by the highest moral good. You must be able to show that the situation was so unique that you had to violate a policy, procedure, process, regulation, law, or ethical rule to do the most moral thing in terms of the ideals of the company and the profession.

If you ever find yourself in such an ethical dilemma, use the following steps:

1. Think through the ethical reasoning process and the concept of the highest moral good.

2. Then, before you take action, ask yourself if you can justify the morality of your actions before a group of your peers and superiors.

3. If you can, then be true to yourself and the principles for which this nation stands or the professional ethical code, and do what you believe is right.

PRACTICAL EXERCISE

I. Identify someone you know who demonstrates strong beliefs, values, and norms.

A. How does this person influence others?

_____

_____

_____

_____

_____

_____

B. Describes this person's influence.

_____

_____

_____

_____

_____

II. What are the four professional values? What does each value mean to you? How does the person from question one model these values?

_____

_____

_____

_____

continued on Page 42

PRACTICAL EXERCISE, continued

III. **Will doing the morally right thing preserve your career? If not, are you prepared to make this sacrifice?**

_____

_____

_____

_____

_____

IV. **Using the ethical reasoning model, work through a complex ethical dilemma from your work setting.**

A. Did you conclude the same answer as those who made the decision?

_____

_____

_____

_____

B. What was the difference, if any, in this outcome versus what actually happened?

_____

_____

_____

_____

SUMMARY

In this chapter, we have examined beliefs, values, and ethics. What you are (your beliefs, values, ethics, and character) is the essence of your ability to lead. Your ability to inspire employees and peers alike to do the right thing, the brave thing, the things they think they cannot do, flows from what you are. Beliefs and values have great motivating power. Under some circumstances, people will die for their beliefs and values. If you are a respected leader of character, you will have significant power to influence the beliefs and values of your employees and peers alike.

As a professional, you are sworn to use that power for the good of *your company*, *your customers*, and *those you lead*.

THE CHARACTER OF A LEADER

> *"A leader, once convinced that a particular course of action is the right one, must be undaunted when the going gets tough."*
>
> RONALD REAGAN

DEFINITION AND EXPLANATION OF CHARACTER

C*haracter* describes a person's inner strength and is the link between values and behaviors. A leader of character does what he believes is right, regardless of the danger or circumstances. A leader's behavior shows his character. In tough situations, leadership takes self-discipline, determination, initiative, compassion, and courage. There is no simple formula for success in all the situations you may face. The key is to remain flexible and attempt to gather as many facts as the circumstances will allow before you must make a decision. When dealing with others, every situation has two sides – listen to both. The way you handle problems depends on the interaction of the factors of leadership (the led, the leader, the situation, and communications).

Character can be strong or weak. A person with strong character recognizes what he wants and has the drive, energy, self-discipline, willpower, and courage to get it. A person with weak character does not know what is needed and lacks purpose, willpower, self-discipline, and courage.

A person who can admit when he is wrong is exhibiting strong character. Some believe that apologizing is a sign of weakness and causes a leader to lose power. Quite the contrary, admitting when you have made a mistake takes humility and moral courage. We are all human and make mistakes. Although placing blame on someone or something else when a mistake is made may be tempting, it indicates weak character, which your subordinates will readily recognize.

We need leaders of strong and honorable character who support the values of loyalty to the nation, the company, and the team: duty, selfless service, and integrity. A leader of character means a person with strong and honorable character.

A *trait* is a distinguishing quality or characteristic of a person. Character is defined as the sum total of an individual's personality traits and the link between a person's values and his behavior. Your character is the combination of personality traits that allows you to behave consistently according to your values, regardless of the circumstances. A person's visible behavior is an indication of his character. When you are in tough situations, you will find that successful leadership takes courage, will, initiative, compassion, and flexibility.

The combination of traits that you need to succeed in the range of situations you will face cannot be simply listed. There are times that you have to be as flexible as a willow. At other times you must be as unyielding as an oak. The combination of character traits that you use in a particular situation depends on the interaction of the factors of leadership and the forces in that situation. Character can be strong or weak.

A person with strong character sees clearly what he wants and has the drive, energy, self-discipline, willpower, and nerve to get it. His traits combine in a synchronized way; they click. A person of strong character attracts followers.

A person of weak character does not know what he wants and lacks purpose, willpower, self-discipline, and drive. His traits are disorganized. He vacillates and is inconsistent. He does not attract followers

It is important to note that a person of strong character can be either moral or immoral. For example, forceful gang leaders are examples of leaders who use their character to pursue immoral values. This type or person has a strong but bad character. Conversely, a person of good or honorable character uses his will and drive to pursue and to build moral values.

PRACTICAL EXERCISE

I. Identify a leader you know.

A. Is his character strong or weak?

_____

_____

_____

B. Is his character good or bad?

_____

_____

_____

C. How does he model his character?

_____

_____

_____

II. How would you define your character?

_____

_____

III. How would your employees, peers, or superiors define your character?

_____

_____

IMPORTANCE OF CHARACTER

Your employees assess your character as they watch your day-to-day actions. They will quickly determine whether you know and enforce the company and professional standards.

Your employees' perceptions of your actions combine to form a continuing assessment of your character. Employees want to be led by leaders who provide strength, inspiration, and guidance and will help them become winners. Whether or not they are willing to trust their careers or lives to a leader depends on their assessment of that leader's courage, competence, and commitment.

Future business success will be won by leaders with strong and honorable character. When mentally preparing for the stress of global competition, it is good to know that ordinary people in the past have shown that kind of character.

Your subordinates assess your character as they see your day-to-day actions:

1. They learn whether you are open and honest with them.
2. They see whether you are indecisive, lazy, or selfish.
3. They may test your will by cutting corners on a job and watching your responses.
4. They observe whether you advance yourself over their interests or whether you are supportive of them and the company.
    a. They will quickly see when your actions are inconsistent with your values or with the formal or informal group norms.
    b. Perceptions of your actions by your employees, peers, and superiors combine to form a continuing assessment of your character.

In stressful situations, everyone wants to follow leaders whom they trust and who provide them strength, inspiration, and guidance. However, if you show character flaws, people will follow you only because of their own sense of duty or your coercive powers. Coercive power will carry you only so far.

Leaders with positive character always produce!

PRACTICAL EXERCISE

I. **Which leader are you?
    And, why do you believe that?**

_____

_____

_____

_____

_____

_____

_____

_____

II. **Who do others say you are?
    And, why do you believe that?**

_____

_____

_____

_____

_____

_____

_____

_____

_____

_____

TRAITS OF CHARACTER

We've covered the definition and importance of character. Now, we will dive into the *traits* of character. What is interesting here is that we all look to our leaders and grade their character on these traits *daily*! These traits are defined from a viewpoint of leadership.

INTEGRITY

Always do what you say you are going to do. In simple form, make and keep promises and commitments. The moment you fail in keeping them is the moment you lose credibility. A word of caution to those who say they are keeping their word but really aren't doing so. When you make and keep promises and commitments, they must be specific and measurable. Otherwise, you are no better than the sifting sands of the sea.

MATURITY

This is the frame by which you lead and make decisions. Are you including enough information and have you thought through prospective outcomes prior to making a decision? Maturity will include wisdom and discernment working together.

WILL

You need the internal strength, or determination, to stand firm on a decision.

SELF-DISCIPLINE

You must have the ability to discipline and train yourself for the present and the future. This can come in the form of not offering an opinion at the time you hear something, but rather waiting to gather more information so that you can make a well-informed and thoughtful decision.

FLEXIBILITY

This is important when gathering information and deciding on available courses of action. This will also help you better frame your decisions and thoughts with your employees. Sometimes, decisions are made in a manner to maintain flexibility of options. It all depends on the situation.

CONFIDENCE

As a leader, you must exude confidence. Do not mistake this for arrogance. There is a difference. You exude confidence through assurance or trust in accomplishing goals and objectives. You do this without being overbearing.

ENDURANCE

Being a leader is like running a marathon. The mantle of responsibility will become a burden that is quite difficult to bear. As a leader, you must have a complete wellness program specifically focusing on the physical, mental, emotional, and spiritual aspects of your life – the complete you!

DECISIVENESS

Whether making a decision or executing a plan, do it with conviction. As a leader, your employees want to know that you will be decisive, although they may not always agree with you. They will respect you because they will know where they stand with you. This is important in building the foundation of trust with your employees.

CALM UNDER STRESS

The old adage that leadership is only tested in a crucible has some merit as it relates to this character trait. As a leader, you will be under stress at all times. That is a given. The level of stress is the only question. Your employees are looking for you to be the one to remain calm. They need reassurance from you that everything is going to be okay. Sometimes that is just a pat on the back or you lending an ear so your employee can vent. Ultimately, your response must be calm.

INITIATIVE

As a leader, you must be bold in taking the initiative. Whether you are leading a new project or line of business or following through with great energy on your portfolio of projects or businesses, it is important to be out front and demonstrate this important trait. Ultimately, you will certainly want your employees to get to that point as well.

JUSTICE

As a leader, you need to make just and right decisions and judgments irrespective of the situation. I want to frame this by saying you should not fall on your saber every single time you perceive injustice being done. Rather, take in the information, frame it up to understand it, and then make a just and right decision or judgment.

SELF IMPROVEMENT

As a leader, you must always strive to improve. Self-improvement comes in many forms such as reading books, taking college courses, participating in seminars, and the like. An active mind also needs an active body. Thus, self-improvement does include how you treat your body as well.

ASSERTIVENESS

Leaders are known to be bold. When the time comes to step forward and boldly stand firm or boldly take a step forward in trying a new strategy, you must do it. Your employees are looking for you to do this. This helps to build confidence, trust, and loyalty in your employees.

EMPATHY OR COMPASSION

As a leader, you must be able to empathize with your employees. They will share things with you about their lives, both work and personal. Because you may have gone through similar situations, you can empathize with them.

Additionally, all good leaders have compassion for their employees. They have a personal interest in seeing them grow and succeed. They also know that employees will fall on hard times for a variety of reasons. They need to know you are there for them.

SENSE OF HUMOR

As a leader, you cannot be so stiff that you are like a robot. You will find it challenging to connect with people. On the flip side, you cannot be the company prankster, either. In having the right balance, you will have a sense of humor to laugh at jokes, laugh at yourself, and not take yourself too seriously.

CREATIVITY

As a leader, you will be charting out strategic direction on the one hand and solving problems on the other. As long as you use consistent frameworks and models, you need to think creatively about the solution.

BEARING

As a leader, you must maintain your bearing. This means always responding with poise to each situation. Make no mistake, this is an expectation whether it's communicated or not.

HUMILITY

As a leader, being humble is important. It demonstrates your willingness to accept others, especially if they are stronger than you in a given area. This is more than mere words. This is action-oriented. Humble leaders are servant – oriented and exude this character trait quite visibly.

TACT

As a leader, you must be actively communicating non-verbally. It means reading your audience, understanding how they are receiving your messages, and being sensitive to their feedback. Some call this political astuteness. Actually, it really is being sensitive to those around you. Being tactful is an others-centered activity.

CHARACTER BUILDING

Building character demands the honesty to determine your own character weaknesses. Ask yourself these questions:

- Have you demonstrated the self-discipline and will upon which strong character is based?

- How have you handled tough situations?

Sometimes you are the best judge of your strengths and weaknesses. Other times you have blind-spots that keep you from seeing your own weaknesses. You must be open to feedback and advice. However, you must take responsibility for continually building and strengthening your character. Others can help, but they cannot do it for you. Also, you are responsible for helping subordinate leaders and employees build their own character.

To build character in yourself or others, you should…

1 Determine as best you can the present situation and status of values and traits.

2 Determine what values and traits you desire to instill. If you are seeking to develop character in others, you should communicate this fact to them. If you don't, it will backfire.

3 Establish an environment that supports the development of the desired values and traits. As a leader, you might make yourself vulnerable within your organization in doing this. It is important that if you do this you protect the environment you have created.

4 Reward those actions which support the desired values and traits, and penalize actions that do not. We will cover positive and coercive motivation tools later in the book. It is important to be consistent and to also be relevant in rewards and penalties.

5 Model the people you want to be like. Be the example for others in terms of the values and traits you want them to have. One of the great learning tools we have as human beings is the ability to mimic or model behavior, actions, attitudes, and the like. This is a great way to help your employees and others that you might influence to see the behavior that you desire from them.

You build character by hard work, study, and challenging experiences. You develop habits of living and working that force you, on a daily basis, to work hard continually to develop your mind and your personality traits.

PRACTICAL EXERCISE

I. How would you rate yourself in terms of being prepared to build character?

_____

_____

_____

_____

_____

II. Are you prepared to face change?

_____

_____

_____

_____

_____

III. Take step one of the build character model.

_____

_____

_____

_____

_____

SUMMARY

In this section, we discussed character as the sum total of your personality traits. It is the link between your values and your behavior. It determines whether you will have the inner strength and tenacity to behave consistently in terms of your values regardless of stress, danger, or consequences. It affects how well you learn and apply critical leadership skills. It is what keeps you going – driving you forward toward your goals – when all other sources of energy and motivation are gone.

Character is the inner power source of leadership and, in this sense, it is the source of all good leadership.

WHAT A LEADER MUST KNOW

> *"Know what you know and know what you do not know."*
> GENERAL GEORGE S. PATTON, JR.

ARNE PEDERSEN

KNOW YOURSELF
"Know thyself"[3]

To lead others successfully, you must know about people and human nature; but before you can understand other people, you must first know yourself. Everyone has strengths and weaknesses. Crucial to your development as a person and a leader is knowing your own strengths and weaknesses. You can then maximize your strengths and work to improve your weaknesses.

The character traits of the previous chapter and questions from the following practical exercise, or PE, will guide you.

These questions are a guide to self-evaluation, so that you can better understand yourself, your personality, your strengths, and your weaknesses.

    I.   Are you an analytical person who likes to work objectively with facts, or are you intuitive, preferring to rely on your instincts and feelings as you make decisions?

    II. Are you warm or cold to the feelings of other people?

    III. Are you introverted, tending to be a loner, or extroverted, relating easily to other people?

    IV. Are your actions directed toward your personal interest, or do you give of your thoughts and time to help others?

    V. Do you prefer a planned, orderly way of life or a flexible, spontaneous one?

There are an abundance of materials, books, articles, etc. on self discovery on the market. While these resources are great ways to help you to better understand yourself, they are certainly not the exhaustive list of available options. If you really want to know more, another option is to seek out an executive coach. Be careful about this option. There are many out there, and only a few who have the academic and professional credentials to really help you.

Before we move on to knowing human nature, let's briefly talk about the Leadership Diagram© on the next page. The following exercise requires concentration. Shut your eyes and think about all the leaders that you have been accountable to in your entire life, including your parents or guardians. Now answer these two questions for each of them: Were they powerful? Did they care about you?

---

[3] Oracle-Shrine of Apollo at Delphi, Greece (6th Century B.C.)

Before you look at the diagram, here is some guidance in using it. If the answer to both of the questions was *yes*, you trusted and respected them. If the answer was *no* to one or both of the questions, then you feared, tolerated, or despised them.

THE LEADERSHIP DIAGRAM©

		DOES HE CARE ABOUT ME?	
		YES	**NO**
IS HE POWERFUL?	**YES**	RESPECTED AND TRUSTED	FEARED
	NO	TOLERATED	DESPISED

Adapted from FM 22-100, Military Leadership, October 1983, p. 142,
Two Key Questions

KNOW HUMAN NATURE

As a leader you will work with followers, peers, superiors, and other people whose support you need to accomplish objectives. You must be able to motivate all these people to support you. To understand and motivate people and to develop a cohesive, disciplined organization, you must understand human nature. People behave according to certain principles of human nature. These principles govern behavior in stressful situations as well as relaxed situations. Stressful situations may release fears that wouldn't normally be evident.

Since all humans react according to principles of human nature, it is important that you study these principles. You must constantly be aware of them through conscientious study. Human nature is the common set of qualities shared by all human beings. We have previously examined some of these qualities – beliefs, values, and character traits – of individuals.

Furthermore, there are many complexities to human nature. As a leader, you need to embrace your employees for who they are. This does not mean that you have to accept poor performance. Rather, it means understanding from a diverse point of view that people are complex and bring a variety of positive and negative attributes to your organization.

Potential for good and bad behavior

All people have the potential for good and bad behavior. One of your most important jobs as a leader is to suppress the bad, bring out the good, and direct that good behavior to the accomplishment of your organization's goals and objectives. Most people want to do the right thing but, unfortunately, many lack the moral fiber or character to behave well under temptation or stress. A leader must realize this and know the conditions that bring out the good and the bad in people. He can then encourage the good and suppress the bad.

Fear

The stress of family life, work life, and the hectic pace of life in general can bring out the bad in people. It can cause a dangerous emotion – *fear*. Fear, if not controlled, can lead to cowardly behavior in an individual or to panic at work. Fear is a common quality of human nature, one that we all experience. Fear causes definite physical reactions.

You can see it in the eyes and sense it in the instability of those experiencing fear. Fear is an emotion that occurs naturally in stressful situations.

What is most important is how a person *handles* fear, and this depends on competence, confidence, and strength of character. Courage is not the absence of fear. It is the ability to act as you believe you should in spite of fear. It is the domination of will over instinct and fear. Competence, and a belief in one's ability to succeed if he tries, are powerful agents in counteracting fear. A person feels fear in direct proportion to his belief that he may fail. As a leader, you can do many things to counteract fear and other types of stress by building competence and confidence in people.

Emotions that contribute to fear

You, the leader, can have an important influence over a variety of emotions such as depression, sadness, feelings of hopelessness, lack of self-worth, and lack of self-respect. These emotions are dangerous in that they breed professional ineffectiveness, fear, and panic.

What is a leader to do? Prevent or control these emotions in yourself by exercising self-discipline. Sense these emotions in your employees and colleagues, and take action to control them. Attack these emotions by setting a positive, cheerful example; talking with individuals and groups; counseling; giving your employees and colleagues a sense of confidence, purpose, meaning, and self-respect.

Emotions that combat fear

To combat fear, panic, and other kinds of stress, you must inspire certain emotions in yourself and your employees. These are feelings of self-worth, self-respect, hope, and confidence – confidence in self, colleagues, and leaders, and that the cause itself is worth working for. Another important emotion is the feeling of being a part of something that is more important than oneself. This is crucial because it leads to cohesiveness in a team.

Human Needs

As human beings, we have a variety of needs such as physical, security, and social. Physical needs include food, shelter, liquids, and sleep. In terms of security needs, people need to feel safe. A leader quickly loses respect if he does not show genuine concern for the physical and security needs of employees and colleagues. And finally, social needs are important motivators, but they are less obvious than physical and security needs. Social needs include the need for self-respect, status, comradeship, love and affection, and the need to belong to a group and to be respected by others in that group.

Higher Needs

There are a variety of higher needs, some of the primary ones being:

RELIGION

From the beginning of recorded history, most people have shown a strong need to believe in God or some other form of higher being. Human beings have a need to explain everything that happens. Science cannot explain everything, and that leaves a mysterious void that people cannot tolerate. Most people need to believe that God exists in some form of higher spiritual being and that this spiritual being has a plan for the universe and an explanation for the many events that cannot be explained by reason and science.

COMPETENCE

We all have a need to be competent and to increase our competence. This is the need to live up to our potential, to be all we can be, to develop all of our talents – whatever they are. It is the need to grow, to become a better, more effective person. When this need is strong in a person, he is motivated toward the achievement of goals. Reaching goals proves to him that he is, in fact, competent and growing in competence. The satisfaction of achieving goals reinforces the need to keep growing by achieving new, more difficult goals.

SERVING A WORTHWHILE CAUSE

Most people will suffer hardship and danger to the degree that they believe the cause or idea is important. All humans need to feel important. We can satisfy this need by being a contributing part of a team that is serving an important cause.

TO BE NEEDED

This need helps explain why some people are motivated to risk their lives to help others, why they will unselfishly serve a cause they believe in, and why they want to be part of an important team. Doing these things gives them the feeling of being needed. We want to be needed by our families, our friends, the leaders we respect, our colleagues, and our society as a whole.

KNOW YOUR JOB

As the leader, you are responsible for knowing the technical and tactical procedures of your job. As previously mentioned, we have a higher need for competence. Intuitively, we feel that we must know our jobs in order to lead our employees effectively. Having this knowledge does not mean that you must be the expert. Rather, you need to know and understand it enough to converse intelligently with the experts you employ.

Technical Knowledge

Your goal is to know every tool, all equipment, etc. that you and your organization use to conduct business. It is a tall order and it calls for technical proficiency, but not necessarily expertise. To obtain this knowledge, you must study and work hard in school, at seminars, and other training opportunities.

Ask your superiors, colleagues, and employees to help you learn. Sometimes, employees make the best instructors. They are proud to show you what they know and to help you learn. Teaching makes them feel intelligent, proud, and important, which they are.

Tactical Knowledge

Besides the technical knowledge to use your organization's tools, templates, techniques, etc. you must know how to employ them. As you are employing them you must do so within the proper business setting to exploit the full advantage in the marketplace. Successful leaders are able to simplify and remove obstacles for their respective organizations to gain advantage in today's complex marketplace.

KNOW YOUR TEAM

If you are to build a disciplined and cohesive organization, you must know your people. This means that you must have a clear understanding of discipline and cohesion. An effective organization is a group of people who know themselves and each other well, care about each other, share mutual trust, respect, confidence, and understanding, and work as a disciplined team to accomplish common goals

Discipline

Discipline exists in an organization when it is orderly, focused, obedient, controlled, and dependable. The character of an organization is a combination of the character of the leaders and the employees who comprise it. If the employees have courage, initiative, will, creative thinking, and self-discipline, the organization will tend to develop a personality, a character, with these traits as its foundations.

Self-discipline means forcing yourself to perform your duties and obligations – what you ought to do – regardless of stress, exhaustion, or other negative conditions in any given situation. Well-disciplined organizations are clearly observable with outcomes such as:

- Goals and objectives are accomplished
- Employees display confidence
- Employees are proud of their organization and perceive its good reputation in the marketplace
- Tools and equipment are always well-maintained and operable
- Employees at all levels are actively engaged in performing their respective duties and functions
- Employees cooperate with one another toward common goals
- Annual business plans, goals, and objectives are well thought out, planned, and executed

Cohesion

Cohesion is the existence of strong bonds of mutual respect, trust, confidence, and understanding among members of a group. Cohesion and discipline are intertwined. If an organization is to be disciplined, it must be cohesive. Cohesion results from the respect, confidence, caring, and communication that bind members of an organization together – mentally, emotionally, and spiritually.

The level of cohesion depends upon how well the organization can work as a smoothly functioning team to achieve goals and objectives. Caring is an essential element of the bonds of cohesion among all employees, including leaders, of an organization. An employee's courage and will in stressful situations are strengthened by his belief that his leader and his colleagues will try to help him because they care for him.

SUMMARY

In this chapter, we have learned some of the key things a leader must know if he is to understand the four factors of leadership. We covered what you must know about yourself, human nature, your job, and your people. This knowledge is fundamental to the development and application of your crucial *be*, *know*, and *do* leadership attributes.

Invisible threads weave together the overall *be*, *know*, and *do* attributes of a leader. In Sections II and III, we covered the essential of "being the" foundation of a leader — values, ethics, and character.

In this section, we covered the essential knowledge that is built on the bedrock of a leader's values and character. What a leader does — the application of his skills — flows from his "being" and "knowing" foundation. It is to these crucial leadership action skills — what they are and how you can learn and apply them — which we now turn.

LEADERSHIP THAT PROVIDES DIRECTION

*"No good decision was ever
made in a swivel chair."*
GENERAL GEORGE S. PATTON, JR.

DECISION-MAKING MODEL

In this chapter we will address the thinking aspects of leadership. We explore how to be a creative, logical thinker. Your thinking skills are called directive skills because they set the direction for your organization.

These skills provide vision, purpose, and goal definition. They are your eyes to the future, allowing you to sense the need for change, when to make it, and how to manage it. As a leader you must continually analyze the situation, identify the problems and their real causes, make decisions, and plan.

These thinking skills are crucial to developing a disciplined and cohesive organization. Thinking skills explained in this section include *identifying, analyzing, and solving problems; making decisions; planning; and goal setting.*

We are going to cover the formal decision making model that shows all of the important work that goes into making decisions. This model is strategic in nature and serves as the strategic plan from which the tactical, situational decisions are made.

Like any good strategic planning, the primary keys to success are research and innovation. This is where most leaders fail because it takes time and discipline to execute.

The steps are simple enough; however, they do require discipline, innovation, flexibility, and creative thinking. From identification of the problem to gathering information to developing courses of action to the final decision, this is the thorough approach to decision making.

DECISION MAKING MODEL

STEPS

1	Identify the Problem	Distill down to salient point
2	Gather Information	Must be relevant and meaningful
3	Develop Courses of Action	Always develop three (3) courses of action
4	Analyze and Compare Courses of Action	Cost-benefit analysis
5	Make a Decision; Select a Course of Action	Be firm and fair
6	Make a Plan	The plan must include contingencies
7	Implement Plan	Communicate, Coordinate, Supervise & Evaluate

PLANNING

Flexibility of Mind

The ability to make appropriate changes in decisions and plans requires a certain flexibility of mind, a crucial trait of a good problem-solver and planner. Here are some key points to keep the mind flexible.

1. Be prepared and anticipate change. This keeps you sharp and less apt to get caught off guard.

2. Think of as many "what ifs" as you can. This will help you to see problems from a variety of angles, not just your own. Most importantly, this might just help you solve a problem that you couldn't otherwise.

3. Prepare for them. Preparation is one of the keys to success. Good preparation makes tactical decision making look natural.

4. Don't be surprised! If you have truly thought through problems and looked at them from multiple viewpoints, you shouldn't be surprised. However, a surprise may linger around the corner only because you didn't have enough information to make a reasonable assumption. Candidly, if you are surprised, don't let your emotions take over! Quickly recover by understanding this surprise and fit it properly into your plans.

5. Make plans to counteract events that might undermine accomplishments. Plan ahead to keep obstacles out of the way.

Objectivity and Intuition

After you have objectively and logically analyzed possible courses of action in a situation using all available information, consider your intuitions and emotions. Are the courses of action consistent with professional values?

The decision-making process is not a purely objective, rational, mathematical formula. The human mind does not work that way, especially under stress. Since the decision-making process is a thought process, it is both rational *and* intuitive. Your intuition is that aspect of your mind that tells you what "feels" right or wrong. Your *intuition* flows from your instincts and your experience. However, never make the mistake of making decisions guided totally by emotions or intuitions and immediately doing what "feels" right. This is a prescription for *disaster*.

Impact of Character

Character has a strong impact on a leader's judgment and application of the decision-making framework. Correct use of the tools, templates, and frameworks, such as the decision-making model, is critical. However, without the character to control fears and deal with reality, and without clear thinking and good judgment, these aids will not be effective.

GOAL SETTING

Goal setting is a critical part of leadership; it determines the direction for your organization. When you assume a leadership position, you should ensure that you and your employees have a set of clearly written goals and policies which you all understand and support.

When setting goals for your organization, remember these key points:

1. Goals are realistic and attainable. Can a reasonable human being with the appropriate skill attain the goals?

2. Goals lead to improved performance and readiness. This is your way of helping your employees truly grow professionally and personally.

3. Involve your employees in the goal-setting process. Do this and they will have ownership.

4. Goals are established, as a minimum, for performance, discipline, morale, cohesion, and employee development.

5. Develop a program or set of policies to achieve each goal. This means your team is working together to develop and establish the programs and policies to execute.

SUMMARY

In this chapter, we have focused on the thinking and directional skills critical to leadership. These skills literally set the direction for your organization. The correct application of these skills is complex and difficult, requiring knowledge, good judgment, and character. In the next chapter, we will walk through implementation and communication.

LEADERSHIP THAT IMPLEMENTS

"*Never tell people how to do things.
Tell them what to do and they will
surprise you with their ingenuity.*"
GENERAL GEORGE S. PATTON, JR.

COMMUNICATION

Definition

Communication is the exchange or flow of information and ideas from one source, or person to another. The process of communication involves a sender transmitting an idea to a receiver. Effective communication occurs only if the receiver understands the exact information or idea that the sender intended to transmit. Communication coordinates and controls all parts of an organization so that they act harmoniously. When you coordinate and supervise, you help each part of your team to reinforce the efforts of accurate timely information. Such information flows from person to person to person – through the bonds of trust, respect, confidence, and understanding. These bonds connect people in a cohesive, coordinated organization.

Examination

Examining the communication process is useful because you coordinate, supervise, evaluate, teach, coach, and mentor through this vital process. The Leadership Communication Model below is fairly simple. The sender encodes ideas, information, or feelings and sends them off in a message. The receiver decodes the message and tries to understand the communicated idea, information, or feeling and then provides feedback. This is going on the assumption that the receiver actually receives the message. We've all experienced someone not listening to us at some point in time. As a leader, it is imperative to listen and understand what is being communicated to you. I encourage you to practice with this model to better understand how your employees are framing up, or encoding, their ideas, information, or feelings and sending them to you.

THE LEADERSHIP COMMUNICATION MODEL©

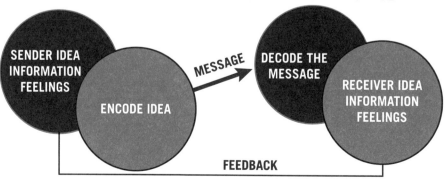

Adapted from FM 22-100, Military Leadership, October 1983, p. 188.

Application of the Leadership Communication Model

The communication process is complex. Let us say that you are a director talking with a manager. You are the sender, the manager is the receiver. Your exchange of information has three parts:

Message – the concept, idea, information, or feelings

Content – the actual words or symbols

Context – the way you deliver the message: your tone of voice, the look in your eye, your state of emotion (anger, fear, uncertainty, coolness or confidence)

The first two parts of the message are generally understood by most people, but the *context* is often not fully appreciated.

As one communication expert explains: "It includes what is not said; it also includes shades of meaning and emphasis; and it even includes ambiguities into which people can read whatever fits their preconceptions best." [4]

Barriers to Effective Communication

Anything that prevents understanding of the exact concept or information intended by the sender is a "barrier" to communication. Many physical and psychological barriers to communication exist. You must understand them and overcome them.

PHYSICAL BARRIERS

Noise, distance, and any other physical factors that distract the attention of the sender or receiver are physical barriers to communication.

PSYCHOLOGICAL BARRIERS

These are more difficult to identify and overcome than physical barriers. You must apply your knowledge of values, character, and human nature to identify and overcome psychological barriers to communication. Some of these barriers are a difference in level of employment , failure to listen, tendency to withhold information, lack of trust, respect, and confidence, and framing of information.

TIPS ON AVOIDING OR OVERCOMING BARRIERS

What are some good tips to avoid or overcome these barriers? Sense what various people (superiors, peers, employees) need to know to do their job. Understand how stress affects communication. Teach and demand accurate

---

[4]Saul W. Gellerman, "Motivation and Productivity" p. 224

reporting in your organization. "Aim at your target before you shoot your message." Know your audience and communicate from their perspective, or frame it for them to understand.

There are several channels of communication to use and to repeat important information (chain of command, informal groups, and informal conversations).

- Communicate to key employees all at one time. This helps to get the message out once and won't get confused by a variety of interpretations that get shared throughout your organization.

- Communicate to the whole organization so that they are completely informed on goals and objectives. Again, this is a great technique to transmit the message and be clear on what it is. All leaders throughout an organization must be clear and consistent with their communication.

- Conduct a personal reconnaissance (face-to-face or walk about). I am a huge fan of this. This is important for two reasons. First off, you really do get to check on how the message was received and correct any misconceptions that exist. Secondly, you can further connect with your employees in a special way face-to-face. If you are in a virtual environment, you need to schedule this time with your employees. It is a must. Virtual teams are harder to lead than those in person. Therefore, you must take extra time to take care of those who do not work in your physical environment.

- Ask questions to ensure that accurate information flows laterally as well as up and down. Listen and take notes. We will be covering the journal in a later chapter. Safe to say that your journal should be with you and be written into during communications whether they are in person, such as the face-to-face, or virtually. We will cover accountability in a later chapter that will speak to these notes and approaches.

COORDINATION

Coordination is defined as "to bring into a common action, movement, or condition; to regulate and combine in harmonious action." All players must be harmonized – singing from the same sheet of music. Plans include a detailed organization of tasks that must be done, who will do them, when, where, how, and why.

All tasks are assigned priorities and owners.

Coordination with superiors, colleagues, employees, and other stakeholders all play an important role in accomplishing goals and objectives from the plan. The best coordination takes place face-to-face. However, you may need to coordinate virtually using a variety of tools and techniques.

Ultimately, the manner in which you carry out coordination is critical. Everyone is busy with their own plans, problems, tasks, objectives, etc. You cannot expect them to stop everything and react to your every wish. *It is inappropriate and self-serving.* You get much better support if you have a "requesting" rather than a "demanding" attitude.

The next time you need to coordinate with various stakeholders, think about how you are communicating and what message they will receive. It will help you overcome the barriers to successful implementation of strategies and plans.

SUPERVISION AND EVALUATION

Supervision

Supervision is defined as keeping a grasp on the situation and ensuring that plans and policies are implemented properly. Supervision includes giving instructions and inspecting continuously, firsthand, the progress of a task.

There is a narrow band of adequate supervision. On one side of the band lies oversupervision. This stifles initiative, breeds resentment, and lowers morale and motivation. And on the other side lies undersupervision. Ultimately, inadequate supervision can lead to miscommunication, lack of coordination, disorganization, and the perception by employees that the leader does not care. This perception can also lead to resentment, low morale, and poor motivation. All employees benefit from appropriate supervision by leaders with more knowledge and experience who tend to see the situation more objectively.

Evaluation

Evaluations are an important part of supervision and are defined as judging worth, quality, or significance of people, ideas, or things. It includes looking at the way people are accomplishing a task. It also includes all types of direct checking and inspecting.

It means getting feedback on how well something is being done and interpreting that feedback. Does the feedback indicate the plan will succeed? Does it indicate the need for modification or a major change in plans or policies?

A routine system is necessary for checking and double-checking the things that are important to cohesion, discipline, morale, team effectiveness, and goal achievement. Checking is such a simple word and concept. It is obvious that leaders must check, but human nature can cause us to overlook the simplest things, which can lead to disaster.

Some people say, "Worry about the little things and the big things will take care of themselves." Yet, others will say, "Worry about the big, important things and don't sweat the small stuff." Neither adage is a good guideline!

First, be concerned about the big things. That is where you exercise most thinking and directional skills. Next, check the little things that make the major things happen.

To anchor this point, think about examples of both poor guides and their probable outcomes. Now, write down an example that uses a balanced approach. What did you learn from this exercise? What will you change in your own behaviors?

_____

_____

_____

_____

_____

_____

_____

Checklists

There are some simple steps in the evaluation process that include using checklists. Many of us have poor memories when it comes to details. We all need checklists of some sort. The more there is to do the more stress there is, and the less time there is available, the more we need checklists. Various approaches, tools, and techniques are available to you.

In managing a project, use the functionality of the tools for the checklists. Another tool is MS Outlook. The task tab can serve as your electronic checklist. Another tool is a journal, such as the type you can buy at a bookstore. Since you are already recording your day, making notes, tracking expenses, and the like in the journal, you can also use it for checklists. Finally, you may have a Standard Operating Procedure checklist as part of your policies and procedures.

Always remember, once you have accomplished an item on your checklist, be sure to always follow through. The rule of thumb is to follow through on your coordination, supervision, and evaluation. As a leader, you need your own system of informal and formal inspections. This will serve as an important source of knowledge about readiness (competence, motivation, etc.).

Good supervision and evaluation require you to be a skilled inspector with a critical, observant eye for detecting those details that can help or hinder goal achievement. Ensure that you take notes. This will help you during reviews (performance, projects, etc.).

PRACTICAL EXERCISE

I. Consider and write down the various approaches to supervision and evaluation.

_____

_____

_____

II. For your organization, what is most important about supervision and evaluation?

_____

_____

_____

III. What works best in your environment? Why?

_____

_____

_____

IV. What are the tools available to you today? Do you use them? Why or why not?

_____

_____

_____

V. What commitments will you make to be better?

_____

_____

_____

SUMMARY

In this chapter, we focused on the implementing skills of leadership – communicating, coordinating, supervising, and evaluating. You can have a great plan and a highly cohesive, disciplined organization. If communication breaks down, however, and if the implementation of the plan is not coordinated, supervised, and continually evaluated, disaster can result. Little things must be checked and double-checked.

Keep in mind that thinking skills, implementing skills, and motivating skills (next chapter) are intertwined and that you must apply them simultaneously as you lead. Obviously, you must think when you communicate, coordinate, supervise, and evaluate. Also, you must understand people and apply your implementing skills in a way that motivates.

LEADERSHIP THAT MOTIVATES

"Perpetual optimism is a force multiplier."
GENERAL COLIN POWELL

n this chapter, we will learn about motivation and illustrate how you can motivate people. We will build on the knowledge you have gained from the previous chapters, since motivational skills flow from your other leadership attributes. This chapter focuses on the development of the principles of motivation. We will also discuss positive and coercive tools of motivation, and teaching and counseling.

MOTIVATION – DEFINITION AND COMMENTARY

A person's *motivation* is a combination of his desire and energy directed at achieving a goal. Motivation is the cause of action. Influencing people's motivation means getting them to want to do what you know must be done. A basic knowledge of human nature is important to understanding motivation.

A person's motivation depends on two things: the strength of certain needs and the perception that taking a certain action will help satisfy those needs. When hungry, you desire food. Satisfaction of this need depends on motivation. The degree of motivation to reach your goal – to obtain food – is affected by how hungry you are and by your perception of the value of the goal.

For example, perhaps you are slightly hungry, but you do not like fish. Someone suggests you go out for a fish dinner. You have a weak need (hunger) and perceive the value of the goal (fish) as low. You are not highly motivated, therefore, to have a fish dinner.

Suppose, however, you are very hungry, you enjoy steak, and someone says he will buy you a steak dinner. You now have a strong need (hunger) and you perceive the value of the goal (steak) as high. Your motivation to get the steak will be high.

People can be motivated by beliefs, values, self-interest, kindness, fears, needs, worthy causes, and other forces. Some of these forces are internal such as needs, fears, and beliefs; some are external such as danger, the environment, chance for promotion, pressure from a superior or an employee, or pressure from family life.

External and internal forces combine to determine what a person is motivated to do in a given situation. The most powerful form of lasting motivation is self-motivation. Your goal as a leader should be to create *self-motivation* in your employees. A few will always require an external coercive force. Most people, however, can become self-motivated if you *teach* them the leadership attributes you learned in this book. Nearly all self-motivated professionals are influenced to some degree by the need to seek job security, promotion, and approval of their colleagues and superiors.

However, the primary influences on a self-motivated professional are internal forces – his values, ethics, and character traits that form the principles by which he lives. A self-motivated professional has moral principles. A moral principle is but a word until it is tested. A professional behaves according to his principles, regardless of the situation. The main reason he fulfills his duty is not to gain a reward or avoid punishment of some sort, but simply to feel satisfied that he is doing the right thing.

PRINCIPLES

Fourteen practical principles (guidelines) flow from this basic view of motivation. We will cover each of these general rules and give you guidance on practical techniques for applying them.

PRINCIPLE 1 – Make the needs of individuals in your organization coincide with the organization's mission, goals, and objectives.

PRINCIPLE 2 – Reward individual and group behavior that supports the organization's mission, goals, and objectives.

PRINCIPLE 3 – Counsel or punish employees who behave in a way that is counter to the organization's mission, goals, and objectives.

PRINCIPLE 4 – Always set a good example.

PRINCIPLE 5 – Develop morale and espirit de corps in your organization

PRINCIPLE 6 – Give your employees tough problems and challenge them to resolve them.

PRINCIPLE 7 – Have your employees participate in the planning of upcoming events.

PRINCIPLE 8 – Alleviate the causes of personal concerns your employees may have so that they can concentrate on their jobs.

PRINCIPLE 9 – Ensure your employees are properly cared for and have the tools they need to succeed.

PRINCIPLE 10 – Keep your employees informed about objectives and performance standards.

PRINCIPLE 11 – Use positive peer pressure to work for you and your organization.

PRINCIPLE 12 – Avoid using statistics as a major method of evaluating departments and motivating employees.

PRINCIPLE 13 – Make the jobs of your employees as challenging, exciting, and meaningful as possible.

PRINCIPLE 14 – Do not tolerate any form of prejudicial talk or behavior in your organization, including sexual harassment.

One of the ways you can help your employees be more successful, especially as you build self-motivated professionals, is to help them understand the varying degrees of responsibility within your organization. Generally speaking, there are two distinct levels of leaders, Director Level and above, and First Line Supervisors and Managers. Helping employees understand various responsibilities will strengthen their stakeholder network, internal and external to your organization, and to accomplish goals and objectives.

The Leadership Responsibility Grid is a great tool to help your employees understand where leaders fit into the overall structure and strategy of a company. Leaders also need to know these responsibility levels so that they don't overburden, or even under-burden themselves.

THE LEADERSHIP RESPONSIBILITY GRID

Director Level	First Line Supervisors and Managers
Commands, establishes policy, plans and programs the work of the organization	Conducts the daily business of the organization within established orders, directives, and policies
Concentrates on strategic level planning and execution	Concentration on tactical level planning and execution
Primarily involved in operations, planning, and related activities	Primarily involved in work of individuals and teams
Concentrates on organization effectiveness and readiness	Concentrates on individual and team work. Ensures high motivation and readiness at this level
Pays particular attention to the standards of performance, leadership and professional development of supervisors and managers	Concentrates on standards of performance and professional development of employees
Creates conditions—makes resources available and removes objectives—so supervisors and managers can do their jobs.	Gets the job done

POSITIVE AND COERCIVE TOOLS

One of the most difficult problems that all leaders face is finding the appropriate mix of the "carrot" and "stick" – the positive and coercive tools of motivation. How do you determine the right combination for various situations? When should you use the carrot and when should you use the stick? This is a difficult but crucial question. Your ability to use an appropriate combination of positive and coercive tools of leadership will have a significant effect on the motivation of your employees and the discipline, cohesion, and effectiveness of your organization.

The Major Positive Tools of Motivation

There are a variety of major positive tools for motivation. Each employee needs different motivation techniques at different times for different purposes.

The most obvious tool is setting the example. This is based on your integrity. You do what you say you are going to do. An example of this is the ever popular, "work-life balance." We've all heard it. As leader, you need to set the example and actually do it. By doing so, you give your employees permission to follow suit and provide some general boundaries or guidelines for them to better understand what you expect.

The one tool that is overplayed and under-delivered is establishing clear goals and standards. However, this is an extremely effective tool if it is used correctly. Remember the chapter on communication which refers to framing conversations and information that you share with your employees. When you establish clear goals and standards, make sure that everyone understands. A great way to do that is to have each employee write in their own words what it means and how it applies to them. You will be amazed at what you learn. At this point, you can customize your message to each employee as they need it framed.

Another set of intuitive tools is teaching, coaching, and counseling. This is important in the development of your employees. This must be practiced daily, weekly, and monthly. Candidly, if you cannot teach, coach, or counsel, you really need to think twice about being in a leadership role.

Some of the most underutilized and misunderstood set of tools are listening, persuading, and rewarding. The biggest reason leaders are not connected with their employees is failure to listen. They are so focused on the fires they need to immediately put out that they don't notice how disconnected they truly are. Thus, listening is a powerful tool in understanding, connecting, and motivating your employees. Another reason for disconnectedness is the inability on the part of leaders to understand how to reward their employees. Again, connectivity with your employees is the key to success. How do you reward your people? Make sure the reward is consistent with the action taken and that the reward is relevant to the individual whom you are rewarding.

Making jobs challenging and meaningful are underused in the market today. These tools do help to develop and grow your employees. Know how far to push your employees. Also, meaningful challenges means that you know your employees and understand how they want to grow and progress. The challenges in and of themselves are relevant and meaningful to each individual employee. These same concepts apply to the team overall.

As a leader, making organizational and employee needs coincide when possible is a great goal to achieve. There are a variety of forces at play such as economic, political, social and religious. These forces need to coincide in order to build the *espirit de corps* that you strive for.

The Coercive Tools of Motivation

There are a variety of coercive tools of motivation at your disposal. These tools must be used sparingly yet efficiently. Verbal and written reprimands (warnings) are the most common of these tools. With no accountability or even overuse, they lose relevance and you will begin to lose your best employees. Warnings about inappropriate behavior need to be coupled with specific instruction on what is appropriate or model behavior.

The final coercive tool, administrative action/discipline, is needed in situations where the employee is just not a good fit and they refuse to leave on their own accord. Be careful not to use this for political gain. It will send a signal to your best employees that you are unwilling to connect and lead. It says that you are willing to cut employees without regard.

Overusing Coercive Tools

There are several major problems with overuse of coercive tools of motivation.

Coercive tools depend upon fear. People have deep security needs to avoid pain and fear-producing situations. These are lower-level needs. Unlike higher-level needs which reinforce motivation, when lower needs are met, motivation to do the job ceases.

People motivated by coercive methods only do enough to reach minimum standards and to avoid punishment by the leader. When the coercive leader is not present to threaten, motivation to reach the leader's standards and goals stops. If discipline is a measure of what employees do when their manager is not present, then in the case of the coercive leader's organization, true discipline is missing.

Improper use of coercive motivation causes resentment and loss of respect for the leader. It creates a negative climate that damages the employees' trust in their leaders. Loss of trust destroys open, candid communication – the organization's life blood. If employees are afraid of a leader, they will be afraid to ask for clarification of messages. They will be afraid to use their initiative, creative intelligence, and judgment in difficult situations when the leader cannot be reached.

Overuse of coercion creates a shallow, false discipline in an organization because the discipline is caused by fear, not by internal forces that carry on in any given situation.

Appropriately using Coercive Tools

We have discussed the perils of overusing coercive methods. When is it appropriate to use coercive tools and how do you use them? When reasonable, attainable standards are set, the leader should communicate the consequences for not attaining minimum standards. In other words, hold people accountable for results. The results must be reasonable and attainable.

Use the following guidelines when thinking through problems and determining how to motivate people in various situations:

- Use positive tools of motivation first with groups of employees and with individuals.

- Strive to instill professional values and character traits in all of your employees. They will then be more likely to be self-motivated by their own professional beliefs, values, and character.

- Determine the cause when an employee or group of employees does not reach a standard. Was it a communication gap, lack of competence, intentional or willful failure?

- To determine fair disciplinary measures, seek the advice of superiors, trusted colleagues, and others whom you trust.

- Use the problem-solving framework to determine an appropriate, fair punishment, and administer it.

- Follow up with evaluation of the effect of your action on the individual and the organization.

- Continue to counsel, evaluate, and take action as appropriate.

TEACHING AND COUNSELING

We have discussed direct, short-range techniques for influencing motivation and how to determine the correct mix of positive and coercive tools of motivation. We discussed that you would do well to improve your skills in applying the positive tools of motivation. Teaching and counseling are positive tools that have an indirect, but powerful effect on motivation. If you teach and counsel well, you will affect your employee's values, character, knowledge, skill, and confidence – positive motivating forces. Furthermore, you will counteract fear and unprofessional values and character traits which are counterproductive motivational forces.

Teaching

Teaching is helping to create the conditions that cause someone to learn and develop. If you are going to influence the competence and motivation of your employees, you must be a skilled teacher. Coaching, counseling, rewarding, and taking appropriate disciplinary measures are all a part of teaching. You must be a good teacher to plan and execute your business effectively and to help your employees develop professionally and personally.

A clear understanding of how people learn is fundamental to being a good teacher.

People learn by the examples of others, by forming a picture in their minds of what they are trying to learn, by gaining and understanding necessary information, and by application or practice.

Learning requires certain important conditions, some more intuitive than others. Candidly, the person must be motivated to learn. If they are not, chances are they will be a disruption to the training process. If it is legally mandatory to attend training, you will need to make do. Involve your employees in the process of learning. This is the adult education style of learning. A few rules of thumb to help you be successful in doing a training seminar or class include the following:

Lecture for 30 minutes or less.

Do a practical exercise.

Take a 10 minute break every hour (50 minutes of instruction and 10 minutes of break).

I want to couch this section of the book by saying there are a variety of approaches to teaching that work just fine. This is an approach that I have used and have found it to work very effectively.

Counseling

Hand in hand with your responsibilities as a teacher are your responsibilities as a coach and a counselor. It is critically important that you counsel all your employees frequently on their professional and personal strengths and weaknesses and on any problem areas that you may be able to help them with.

Counseling is talking with a person in a way that helps that person solve a problem or helps to create conditions that will cause the person to improve his behavior, character, or values. Counseling is a leadership skill that is a composite of leading and teaching. Good counseling, like good teaching, requires a combination of all your leadership *be, know,* and *do* attributes.

Counseling requires…

…directional (thinking) skills – such as identifying the problem, analyzing the factors and forces influencing the behavior of the employee being counseled, and planning and organizing the counseling session

…implementing skills – coordinating the session as it proceeds

…an understanding of human nature – what causes the employee to behave in a counterproductive manner and what will be required to change his behavior, character traits, or values

…sincerity, compassion, and kindness

…a sense of timing – when to let the counselee make his own decisions and when you should make them for him, when to be kind and understanding, and when to be firm and unyielding

SUMMARY

In this chapter, we focused on practical techniques for increasing an employee's motivation to achieve standards of performance and business objectives. We defined motivation and explained a basic view of what motivates people – the perception that taking specific actions will lead to the satisfaction of certain needs. We further learned a number of important principles of motivation and provided you practical, direct techniques for applying the principles. Finally, we discussed teaching and counseling – two leadership skills that have an indirect, yet powerful, long-range impact on the motivation of your employees.

LEADER PROGRAMS

> "There is no victory at bargain basement prices."
> DWIGHT D. EISENHOWER

LEADERSHIP SELF-DEVELOPMENT

In the first chapter, we defined leadership as the process through which a person influences others to accomplish objectives, goals, tasks, etc. We covered the four major factors of leadership: the follower, the leader, communication, and the situation. We then walked through what a leader must *be* (beliefs, values, ethics, character), *know* (self, job, organization), *do* (direct, implement, motivate) to accomplish objectives, goals, task, etc.

To improve yourself and your employees, you should strive to learn more about the four factors of leadership and how they affect each other. You should also seek to improve yourself in the areas of what a leader must *be, know*, and *do*. Good leaders have a never-ending passion to increase their competence as people and as leaders through study and experience.

A good leadership self-development program should include a combination of the following:

- Seek additional responsibility and tough, challenging jobs. You build character, knowledge, and skills by handling tough jobs and situations. This is mandatory if you want to further develop your leadership skills.

- Engage in self-study: industry history, industry publications, economics, etc...Sometimes joining the local symphony and experiencing symphonies, operas and the like will help you to break out of your traditional mold and learn new ways of approaching various people.

- Take supplemental courses in addition to any CE (continuing education) that you are required to complete. Courses might include organizational behavior and development, management, literature, and etc... College level courses or required CE can enhance your competence as a leader.

Furthermore, you must write your own leadership development program. You must do this or you will not develop as a leader. You are encouraged to do so with the assistance of your trusted advisors (superiors, colleagues, and others). For those of you who want to learn more about how to do this, you can contact my company, Human Capital Management (www.hcm-llc.com) and schedule one of our courses for your organization.

Every six months update your program based on your increased knowledge and development.

The next few steps are a guide to developing your program:

STEP 1: IDENTIFY YOUR STRENGTHS AND WEAKNESSES IN THE FOLLOWING AREAS:

- Beliefs, values, and ethics
- Character traits
- Knowledge (yourself, human nature, your job, your organization)
- Directional skills (problem-solving, planning, decision-making, goal-setting)
- Implementing skills (communicating, coordinating, supervising, evaluating)
- Motivating skills (teaching, counseling, and otherwise applying the principles of motivation)

STEP 2: SET GOALS:

- Learn more about human needs
- Improve ability to apply principles of motivation
- Improve communication skills
- Improve teaching skills
- Improve counseling skills

STEP 3: DEVELOP PLANS TO ACHIEVE GOALS:

- Goal A: Learn more about human needs
- Goal B: Improve ability to apply the principles of motivation
- Goal C: Improve communication skills
- Goal D: Improve your teaching skills
- Goal E: Improve your counseling skills

STEP 4: EVALUATE. FOR EACH GOAL WRITE OUT TWO OR MORE WAYS OF EVALUATING PROGRESS TOWARD ACHIEVEMENT:

- Self-evaluate

- Seek feedback from trusted resources (Superiors, colleagues, employees)

- Look at your scores on your Continuing Education courses. These are indications of progress toward goals.

IN REVIEW, YOUR LEADERSHIP SELF-DEVELOPMENT PROGRAM CONSISTS OF FOUR MAJOR STEPS:

- Identify your strengths and ways you want to improve your *be, know,* and *do* attributes. Identify your weaknesses and ways you want to better manage them.

- Set a goal for each strength or other attributes you want to improve.

- Set a goal for each weakness you want to better manage.

- Develop a plan to achieve each goal.

- Develop at least one method for evaluating your progress toward each goal.

INDIVIDUAL AND GROUP FEEDBACK

Individual Feedback

Every leader must have a program for systematically counseling and for receiving feedback from his employees. Plan to spend 30 to 60 minutes with each employee every month. You need to ensure that the information shared is confidential. The answers to your questions must be honest and candid.

Here are some sample questions:

- What is motivating you to do you best?
- What can we, as leaders, do to improve the organization?
- How would you rate your morale?
- Do you feel that you are learning and developing as a professional?

This is a great opportunity to counsel and coach your employees on how they can further develop professionally. In order to do this, you must know the individual employee very well. Many great benefits are derived from these sessions, such as identifying problems, learning the perception of employees, and identifying various organizational strengths and weaknesses. From these sessions, you make plans to address opportunities to improve using the frameworks provided.

Group Feedback

This program involves informal talks (i.e. town hall sessions) by the leader with their respective organization in small groups, usually eight or fewer, about organizational accomplishments, problems, strengths, weaknesses, cohesion, discipline, and other professional topics.

All leaders within their respective organizations must carry this out. Each leader needs to plan one (1) hour per month for each small group. If you are planning on doing this on a larger scale such as a functional department or division, you should plan for this quarterly and to spend a few hours (four would be good) with your organization. To keep this under control, set the agenda, set the rules, and enforce those same rules. You as the leader must understand the thoughts, emotions, perceptions, and problems of all levels of employees – *their frames of reference.*

THE JOURNAL

The purpose of the journal is two-fold. The first is to record the details of significant events as they occur or soon afterwards. Timely notes are memory joggers. For example, it is important to take notes during meetings, conference calls, seminars, training, educational opportunities, during business interactions, and during times of contemplation. The second is to brainstorm, storyboard, and flesh out concepts and ideas through journaling.

The notes you take can then be translated into project plans, performance plans, contracts, and the like. This builds in accountability that is important. Additionally, it helps to recall conversations and helps you regain previous thought processes and be prepared to take them to the next logical step.

When needing time to think through proposals, presentations, ideas, and the like, it is important to storyboard your thoughts within your journal. By capturing your thoughts here and collectively organizing them into a storyboard, you now have a record of thoughts, ideas, and approach. **It is a powerful tool to use as a leader and a professional!**

The final importance of the journal is to write out your annual leadership plan in the journal itself. Why? It is designed to be carried with you everywhere and it is in your writing, or framework. You will refer to it from time to time as an accountability to yourself to continue to lead and grow.

THE AFTER ACTION REVIEW

The purpose of the after action review is to literally review the last project, program, sales campaign, surgery, etc. with the actual team who performed it with you to analyze exactly what happened, perceptions of what happened, leader attributes applied or misapplied, take notes for the record, brainstorm and dialog on prospective alternatives for improvement, record them, assign and investigate their value for future operations.

The framework for this process as follows is simple and requires leader discipline to be consistent. There are two models here for a reason. First, you need to know, understand, and be able to execute the AAR Model. Secondly, in order for the AAR to be relevant, you must sequence it. Yes, that is correct. You cannot just throw this up on a whiteboard and walk away. There is a sequence to executing a solid AAR so that it truly becomes the accountability tool that you need.

AAR FRAMEWORK[©]

Planning:
- Review benchmark standards
- Identify when AARs will occur
- Determine who will attend
- Select potential AAR sites
- Choose facilitator aids
- Review the AAR plan

Preparation:
- Review objective, standard operating procedures (SOPs), etc..
- Identify key events that need observation
- Collect observations from leaders
- Organize observations into key discussion points
- Prepare the AAR site
- Conduct rehearsals

Conduct:
Maximum participation
Maintain sequencing
Maintain focus objectives
Record key points

Follow-up:
- Identify task for retraining
- Fix the problem
- Use information to make management assessments

Adapted from TC25-20, A Leader's Guide to After Action Reviews, September 1993, pps. 1-6, The AAR Process

AAR SEQUENCING©

I. INTRODUCTIONS AND RULES.

II. REVIEW OF OBJECTIVES AND INTENT.
- Review objectives
- Review leader's intent
- Review relevant industry and organization procedures

III. SUMMARY OF EVENTS.

IV. DISCUSSION OF KEY POINTS.
- Chronological order of events
- Orgainizational operating procedures
- Key events/themes/issues

V. DISCUSSION OF OPTIONAL POINTS.
- Individual skills/knowledge competance
- Tasks sustain/improve
- Statistics

VI. COMMITMENTS.
- Captured all key points
- Assigned key points
- Agreed upon follow up

VII. CLOSING COMMENTS. *(Summary)*

SUMMARY

In this chapter, we covered a variety of programs that will assist you and your organization in leadership. Use these programs as guides to develop yourself, your colleagues, and your organization.

They have been tried, tested, and work rather well. Use your imagination to apply these and other programs at every opportunity in the daily activities of your organization.

If you do, your organization shall reap the benefits of cohesion, discipline, motivation, and overall effectiveness.

PART 2:
CASE STUDIES

"It is no use saying, 'We are doing our best.' You have got to succeed in doing what is necessary."
WINSTON CHURCHILL

n these case studies, we will be discussing four publicly traded companies. We only name two because the two unnamed stocks might be too volatile because of the size of those companies.

These case studies start from the best to the worst in corporate leadership. The topics range from a leadership center of excellence, to the company vampire, to the leadership gap, to moral and ethical, and finally to acknowledgement of diversity in leadership.

If you recall from earlier in the book, I told you that the employee economic value added, leadership measurement, was the correct measurement for leadership. For those of you who are finance and accounting gurus, the information for this measurement is found in the balance sheet and income statement. Thus, the leadership measurement added is a real financial measurement of leadership.

Furthermore, we need to apply tests to the measurement to validate what the measurement is telling us. The three tests that I developed for this are 1) the slope is positive, 2) the numbers are positive, and 3) the measurement is consistent over time. In order for a company to be called a leadership company, all three tests must be passed. Please keep these three tests in mind as you are reading the case studies and viewing the measurements.

CASE STUDY 1 ——————————————————————————————
LEADERSHIP CENTER OF EXCELLENCE

One of the examples briefly alluded to in the introduction to this book is what Jack Welch did at General Electric (GE). Shortly after he took over the reins of GE, Jack made a very important and historic decision. Leadership would be the core competency of GE. In order to make this happen and truly be pervasive throughout the company, he needed a vehicle to get him there. This vehicle is the center of excellence. Thus, he created the leadership center of excellence for GE. Hundreds, if not thousands, of men and women leaders have gone through this center and have been trained in the GE leadership way. Some have stayed on and have helped to grow GE into the giant it is today. Others have moved on to other ventures and companies and have grown those businesses based upon what they learned at GE.

So, what is a leadership center of excellence and how do you measure it? A *leadership center of excellence* is a program designed specifically to train leaders at all levels of the organization. This includes the various levels of skill and experience. Intuitively, leadership training is ever ongoing. The curriculum will include leader assessments, leadership concepts and principles, ethics, leadership body of knowledge, leadership models and frameworks, and ultimately the accountability to execute.

The program itself is fungible and may be applied across a variety of environments and cultures. It is important to note that the vision, mission, and culture of each company will impact the direction, credibility, and sustainability. The responsibility for these rests squarely on the shoulders of the senior leadership of each company. It is also important to note that not every company can successfully implement a leadership center of excellence. The question then becomes how do I do this successfully? There is no silver bullet per se. However, it is imperative to engage someone who understands all of the tenets of leadership and actually has a program to offer that will add real benefit and value.

Jack Welch invested the time and money to design, develop, and implement a leadership center of excellence. He was a great leader and was mostly influenced by his mother and then by his first boss at GE, Reuben Gutoff, who talked him into staying and promised him an entrepreneurial environment; thus, a star was born. An example of his great leadership is shown for the ten-year period used to calculate the leadership measurement added (1992 through 2001). We also found that ROE increased on average 22.34% per year, the market capitalization increased 436%, and revenues grew 125.9%.

In addition, we have gotten great insight into his style and personality from his autobiography, "Straight from the Gut," and his second book, "Winning." However, what about his legacy? What about the abundance of leaders still in the company? Are they continuing that success? How do you measure that success?

How good is GE with this leadership center of excellence? In the graph below, I have included the public information from the 10K, or annual report, for a ten year period alluded to earlier. The two dimensional graph below depicts the leadership measurement at GE for this decade.

What is important to note, is that the leadership center of excellence and a variety of variables led to passing the three tests of the leadership measurement. The first test is passed because of a positive slope of the leadership measurement over this same period. The second test is also passed in that the numbers are positive. The third test is passed because of the consistency of the leadership measurement. This success is why GE has a pervasive leadership culture and continues to dominate multi-national conglomerate corporations.

LEADERSHIP MEASUREMENT

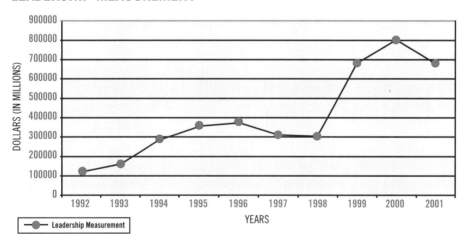

Again, this success is built around a solid leadership center of excellence. The intangibles include a practicable vision, mission, and culture. Finally, senior management not only began this program, they also endorse it strongly. Ultimately, each organization wanting to improve their leadership to increase value, should consider the GE model: leadership center of excellence; supportive vision, mission, and culture; engaged and supportive senior management team.

CASE STUDY 2

THE COMPANY VAMPIRE

What is the number one reason that people leave their current job? According to SHRM, Society of Human Resource Management, it is the immediate supervisor, irrespective of level within the organization. Or is it the company vampire? We will explore what a company vampire is, explore a few things about leaders, and then tie all of this back to our leadership measurement.

Before we get into the definition of what a company vampire is, let's explore a few things about our leaders first. The following exercise does need to be repeated. Now, picture in your mind all of the leaders to whom you have had accountability. It is important that you answer these next two questions honestly. Were they powerful? Did they care about you?

If the answer to both of these questions is *yes*, those were leaders that you

? →	DOES HE CARE ABOUT ME?	
	YES	NO
IS HE POWERFUL? YES	**RESPECTED AND TRUSTED**	**FEARED**
NO	**TOLERATED**	**DESPISED**

trusted and respected. If the answer to one or both of these questions is *no*, those were leaders that you tolerated, feared, or despised. Generally speaking, you will be able to count on one hand the number of leaders whom you trusted and respected. This is not an "*a-ha*" moment. Rather, this is a get real moment. As we discussed previously in the book, there are approximately 10% of the population who are natural leaders. It is their gift and it is second nature for them. We know who they are. We've always known. We knew who they were when we were growing up. We knew who they were when they walked in to a room.

What does that mean for the remaining 90% who are in leadership positions? These folks either do not know or refuse to acknowledge that they are not natural leaders. They abuse power and people. In most cases, they are not even aware of what they are doing. And, in most cases, they are not bad people. They need help to learn how to lead people, *daily*.

With that context in mind, what indeed is a company vampire? A *company vampire* is a person who is in a leadership position, carries great authority within the organization, and is part of the 90% who do not have the natural leadership gift, refuses to acknowledge it, and intentionally engages in abusive behavior. Depending upon the size of the organization, this person is usually operating at a director level or above. This can include the CEO, a board member, or even an owner.

In terms of sustainability, it is imperative to identify these people, attempt to help them change, or eventually help them out the door if they refuse to change. The best way to approach this is to use a skilled third party who can be accountable to you to guide your organization in identifying, training, coaching, teaching, and mentoring these people with a program that has proven measurable success. Using the leadership measurement, we can explore one such company and what has happened with them.

A brief background on this company, which we shall call ABC Company, is that it is a publicly traded company and has an individual on its senior team who is a company vampire. His behavior includes an argumentative style with employees, demeaning and degrading comments to employees, and a generally coercive leadership approach. This person is feared. He has power and does not exercise genuine care for employees.

What we have learned before on the leadership measurement is that with good leadership that is trained and executed daily and all three tests are passed, that company is a leadership company.

So what has happened to the ABC Company?

The slope on the chart below is generally positive in a few of the years, although not all. We can see that the numbers over the eleven year period are negative except for one year. We also see that there is some inconsistency as well. Granted, the inconsistency is not over-dramatic, however, it is inconsistent. What does this mean to this company?

In terms of long-term sustainability, this company is actually in trouble. A deeper dive into the management discussion of the filed 10Ks demonstrates that the only growth is inorganic. This means that something is amiss with the business model and/or how the business model is being executed. Since this trend is consistent over the eleven-year period, companies like ABC Company need to engage a third party trusted advisor who can help them identify, strategize, plan, implement, and execute a strategy to help them either pull out of this current trend or increase the value enough to sell it.

LEADERSHIIP MEASUREMENT

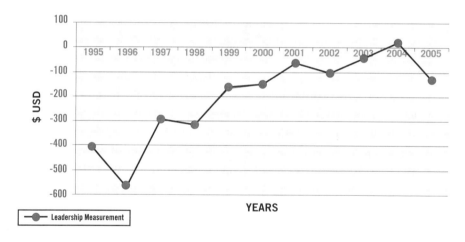

CASE STUDY 3 ————————————————————————————

THE LEADERSHIP GAP

Does your company have a succession plan? What does that plan really mean? Are the people identified really prepared to take on the mantle of leadership for your company? How many Generation X or Generation Y employees are prepared to take that next step? If these questions constantly keep you awake at night, then you are like most executives. Let's explore what this leadership gap is and what it takes to close it. Along the way, we will examine the leadership measurement to demonstrate the need for continuity or improvement in leadership.

SHRM, Society of Human Resource Management, discusses this growing leadership gap as one of the core issues that companies are facing today. So, what is this leadership gap? Where did it begin? What do we need to do to select and prepare the next generation of leaders?

Feeling overwhelmed, join the crowd. Most companies are feeling that way. When we look into the market today, there are a plethora of "leadership" courses for people to take. Unfortunately, they tend to be incomplete by themselves and companies spend thousands, if not millions, of dollars trying to find the "silver bullet."

The "leadership gap" as it is coined really began over a decade ago when Generation X entered the workforce. The workforce had plenty of baby boomers in a variety of roles within companies but this new generation was different. In general, they did not tend to want to take on the mantle of leadership as it was *defined* by the baby boomer generation. In short, they looked at it differently.

They were molded by the distrust of government, the dawning age of micro computers, the concern for global nuclear warfare (the policy of mutual self-destruction), and the rise of "Reagonomics." This is a group that was willing and able to take risks, a new generation of entrepreneurs. They did not care about the same career progression path the baby boomers espoused.

This generation did not have formal leadership training except for those who went into military service. Leadership was learned on the job and tended to be incomplete. In an effort to close the gap, companies have spent millions of dollars in training, seminars, speakers, and the like. If all of the people that went to these training sessions, seminars, speakers, and so on were asked where the material is now, an abundance of them would sheepishly say that it is on a shelf at the office or home collecting dust.

What does that mean? Candidly, it means that this "leadership training" was viewed as nothing more than a "check the block exercise" and not what it was really intended for. Eventually, this led to more frustration for all parties involved and the leadership gap continued to grow.

With that backdrop, let's explore the definition of the leadership gap. The *leadership gap* is a real or perceived void in successive leaders from one generation to another. The word "generation" is generic in this contextual use in that it does not necessarily refer to birth periods. It can be applied to business, community, or political leaders. The void is created by a lack of apprenticeship, training, culture, and understanding. Strategically, it is the difference in viewpoint. Are you more concerned with the month-end or quarter-end results? Or, are you focused more on sustainability over decades and generations? In these two contexts, the strategies present a stark contrast.

At this point, you are probably wondering what you need to do to close the gap. Panicking and spending more money like "drunken sailors" is not the answer. There is a great deal of work around strategy, culture, and commitment that your company must go through before you do anything. Typically, this exercise will be difficult from a human perspective. Before you go down the path of spending even more money on leadership, please ensure that you have done all your homework. It would make sense to find an expert to help you uncover all the data and design the right program for your company.

What does this leadership gap look like from our leadership measurement?

For this case study, we took a look at a mature technology company based in California. Like the previous companies, this is a publicly traded company. And like the previous company, we will keep the company name and individual names confidential.

This mature technology company, whom we shall call "Innotech, Inc.," has been a solid performing company with a plethora of baby boomers in both the leadership roles and individual contributor roles. They have hired Generation X employees and are starting to hire Generation Y employees. They still look at leadership from their own perspective and have not quite made the connection with following generations. Thus, they have a leadership gap that they now must aggressively close for long term sustainability purposes. They do have some leaders who acknowledge this issue and are attempting to work within the current culture and systems to groom this next generation. Unfortunately, it is not considered a strategic issue to be solved at this time.

Let us examine our measurement and see what is going on with this company. You will notice that they are all over the board! In our first test, we notice that the slope is both negative and positive. In the second test, we notice that the numbers are both negative and positive. And the final test demonstrates inconsistency in the cycle but does show a positive trend. Ultimately, this last test demonstrates a lack of consistency in leadership. What this does show is that the "manage up" mantra that is played throughout this company does not provide the necessary consistency and sustainability required to lead it into the future.

LEADERSHIP MEASUREMENT

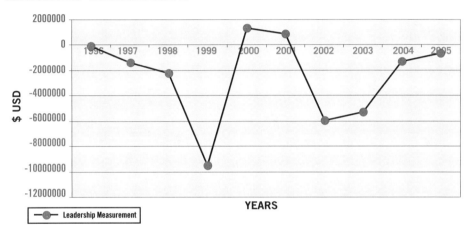

CASE STUDY 4 ————————————————————————————

ETHICS AND MORALS

Is your company making decisions based upon what individuals like, want, or need? Or is your company making decisions in the best interest of the shareholders, the employees, and all other stakeholders? In this case study, we are going to explore some rather "sticky" and deep issues in ethics and morals. These are not the typical discussions that companies have with their various stakeholders for the sake of appeasement. Rather, this exploration will go directly into the root of ethics and morals in leadership and our leadership measurement to demonstrate the seriousness of this topic as it relates to leadership.

These topic items are at the core of the Sarbanes–Oxley law pertaining to disclosure and record keeping. We have seen a plethora of high profile cases of abuse of power that demonstrated a lack of "good" moral and ethical behavior. This begs the question, what is good moral and ethical behavior? Indeed, a society that downplays its moral and ethical behaviors will spiral downward with a lack of true leadership. Before we discuss our case study company, we need to understand more about good moral and ethical behavior as we previously covered in the book

What is at root with this are beliefs, values, and norms. A belief is an assumption or conviction that you hold to be true regarding people, concepts, or things. We all have beliefs about things, concepts, and people. One employee may believe that their obligation to their career simply means putting in time from "8 to 5." Another may believe that obligation is selflessly serving the company, customers, and co-workers. We have beliefs about human nature – what makes people tick. We usually cannot prove our beliefs scientifically, but we think and feel that they are true.

A value is an attitude about the worth or importance of people, concepts, or things. You may place high value on a family heirloom, such as your grandfather's watch or on a clean well-maintained car. You may value personal comfort or freedom to travel. You may value a friend, a relative, or an adult who helped you as you were growing up.

Norms are both formal and informal. Formal norms are official standards or laws that govern behavior. Traffic lights, The United States Constitution, and agreements with customers are formal norms that direct behavior. They dictate what actions are required or forbidden. Safety regulations and codes and company operating procedures are also formal norms.

Informal norms are unwritten rules or standards that govern the behavior of a group of members. The U.S. Army has an informal norm that the wounded are evacuated after a battle, regardless of danger. At the root of this norm is a shared value about the importance of caring for each other. Each member of the Army found comfort in knowing that he would be cared for.

As we take this into context, let us explore a model for ethics. This model is the ethical reasoning model. As you can see in the diagram below, we will have pressures applied upon us as we make decisions. What is important is understanding and consciously applying a consistent model for good moral and ethical behavior, thus the ethical reasoning model.

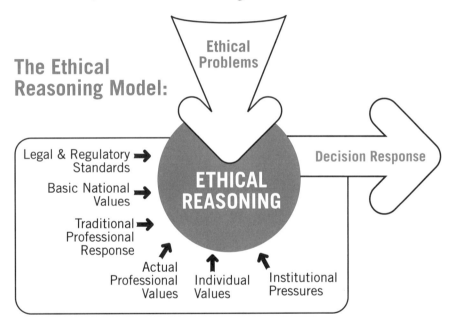

With that contextual background, let's introduce our case study company. Like the companies before, we are looking at a publicly traded company. This one happens to be a high profile company. We know it as Enron Corporation. I know; some of you are saying to yourself, that one is a slam dunk. I encourage you to indulge me.

Early on, the leadership of Enron was fine. No one saw any apparent problems. What did happen, though, is the leadership of Enron acquiesced to the pressures of successfully leading a company and did not consistently apply a good moral and ethical model, such as the ethical reasoning model above. Candidly, many companies do struggle. The solution is to bring someone in who has the capability and experience to implement a model such as the ethical reasoning model to provide the necessary accountability.

We need to apply the standard leadership measurement. As we apply all three tests we can see that Enron is indeed a failure in leadership. The slope is both positive and negative (especially in the end). The numbers are both positive and negative (especially in the end). And, there is no consistency whatsoever. Ultimately, we know the outcome here is a company that is out of business, millions if not billions in lost shareholder value, and several executives convicted of crimes.

The final thought is that good moral and ethical behavior does matter in leadership.

LEADERSHIP MEASUREMENT

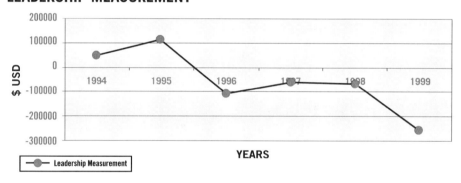

CASE STUDY 5

GETTING REAL: ACKNOWLEDGING, UNDERSTANDING, AND ACCEPTING YOUR PEOPLE

Who are your employees, your people? Where do they come from? What is their socio-economic background? What relationships do they have with their parents, siblings, or friends? What problems have they faced in the past and how have they faced them? These are the various questions many employers and leaders have in their respective hearts about all of their people. How does one actually engage with their people and motivate them to achieve great goals and objectives?

Do these questions all seem to be the age-old questions that you and your organization have been trying to address, understand, and achieve? Join the growing number of companies that are still trying to get their arms around them, make plans, and move forward.

The science and art of the interview process are interesting and measurable indeed. However, what is more telling is that people can and will hide who they are even through the best of the behavioral interviews. Let us be candid with one another. People will do what it takes to get the job they want. Our free market works that way. The challenge for our leaders then becomes how to better connect with their people to better understand how to best position them not only to succeed but to excel.

Previously, we covered values, beliefs and norms. Briefly, beliefs are assumptions or convictions that we hold true regarding people, concepts, or things. Values are attitudes about the worth of people, concepts, or things. Norms are broken down further into two concepts, formal and informal. Formal norms are official standards or laws that govern behavior. Informal norms are unwritten rules or standards that govern the behavior of a group of members.

With this context, we can now explore how you, the leader, can get real with your people. The first step is always to understand that both you and your employees are human beings and need to treat each other with respect. With that understanding in mind, it will now be easier to sit down informally with the person across the table and truly be able to understand and connect with who they really are and not just the façade that you see at work.

A great example of getting real with my people was the first platoon that I commanded. I recall meeting them at Grafenwöhr Training Area for Tank gunnery. Over the next two years I came to know some amazing men, all of whom I am honored to have commanded. The makeup of my platoon was diverse. I will deliver it to you in a few ways. First off, ethnic makeup of my platoon was 56% White, 25% Hispanic, and 19% African American. Secondly, the socio-economic make up of my platoon was 69% middle class, 19% poor, and 19% rich. Religiously, we had 75% Protestant and 25% Catholic for 100% Christian-based religion. This is not to say that everyone actively went to church. Candidly, only 25% to 30% actually went to church regularly irrespective of denomination.

Another breakdown of my platoon is where people hailed from. 87% were U.S. citizens and 13% were non-U.S. citizens. Of course, each man serving in the Army who was not a U.S. citizen could apply for citizenship if they so chose.

For those who were U.S. citizens, 25% came from the Midwest, 19% from both the Mountain Region and the West Coast, and 6% each coming from the North Region, the South Region, the East Region, and a U.S. Territory (Puerto Rico). Furthermore, 63% of my Platoon was Generation X with the balance, 37%, being Baby Boomers.

Intuitively, the idea here is to understand where people hail from and how they frame life. Racial differences play a part as do socio-economic differences, geographical differences, generational differences, etc…

What this boils down to is how you work with your people and how you connect with your people.

Fast-forwarding in my military career, the company I commanded had even more interesting dynamics. Besides the types of dynamics I described above, the other dynamics included the differences in Regular Army, Reserves, and National Guard components. Each saw the mission a bit differently and had a variety of personnel to carry out the missions we were assigned. This also manifested itself in that we had both men and women in this unit. An interesting point of differentiation between the components is the politics. Each component had its own brand of politics and political structures to work through. Additionally, the National Guard had two bosses, the Governor and the President, in that order. Furthermore, these dynamics added complexities to our stakeholdering efforts at battalion, brigade and division level.

How do you cut through all of this to get to the heart of people and influence them to execute and accomplish great objectives or missions? Again, it is about knowing where they come from and how they frame life. As a leader, it is incumbent upon you to know how to communicate with a variety of people. A leader must know how to influence each person to proper and productive action.

One of the most important measurements of my time in the military is how well a unit performed in combat.

As a Platoon Leader, the platoon I commanded successfully closed with and destroyed the enemy in three battles, the third of which has gone down in U.S. Army history as the second largest armor battle, the Battle for Medina Ridge. The brigade my platoon was part of flawlessly executed the air–land battle doctrine. For my efforts as a leader and commander of my platoon, I earned the Bronze Star Medal.

As a Company Commander and a Battalion Plans Officer we trained up the 76th Separate Infantry Brigade for deployment over the course of five years which culminated (after I resigned from the Army) in the 76th SIB successfully deploying to Afghanistan and subsequently redeploying back to Indiana. For my efforts as a company commander and battalion plans officer, I earned several awards and commendations.

So, to wrap up the case studies and this book, which leader are you? Which company do you work at? Are you ready to take the next step in leadership? Do you want to fulfill your potential and help others to do the same?

Follow up on what you have just read by taking a leadership course and implement your leadership plan and skills daily!

I CHARGE YOU TO GO FORTH AND LEAD!

ACKNOWLEDGEMENTS

I would like to thank all of those who have been part of this lengthy and enjoyable project.

Thank you to Jeff Lampe, Rich Smikle, Ken Tracy, and Jim Davis. These men are my company board of advisors and were tremendous in their feedback and guidance.

Thank you also to Neil Crebbe and John Johnson. They are close friends and brothers in this life who challenged me on points throughout the process.

Thank you to Greg Ballard, Lt Colonel (R) U.S. Marines. He graciously shared stories of his own struggles and victories in writing his book and the process for getting it published. I'd have Greg in my foxhole covering me anytime, anywhere!

Thank you to Phil Theiler, my first company commander and U.S. Army Colonel. He was instrumental in my development as a young officer and leader. I'd go to war with him again!

Thank you to Dick Pedersen, Colonel (R) U.S. Army and my dad. He mentored and coached me into the man I am today. He taught the HIL philosophy that he learned from my grandfather, Richard Bert Pedersen, Commander (R) U.S. Navy. This is my family legacy that he charged me to pass down to my children and to pass on to others who would listen and learn.

I would like to acknowledge and thank Petra Ritchie and Neil Crebbe for their editing contributions. They were a big help in making getting this book to market.

I would also like to acknowledge and thank the IBJ for their work as my publisher. As "the" business journal in the state of Indiana, they helped to critically look at this project. They are as particular on which authors they will publish as I am on who I looked to as a publisher. It was a great match.

FOOTNOTES

1   Adapted from FM 22-100, Military Leadership, October 1983, p. 49, Leadership Framework *(Page 17)*

2   Adapted from FM 22-100, Military Leadership, October 1983, pps. 98 and 99, Ethical Reasoning Process *(Page 39)*

3   Oracle-Shrine of Apollo at Delphi, Greece (6th Century B.C.) *(Page 61)*

4   Saul W. Gellerman, Motivation and Productivity, p. 224 *(Page 78)*

FRAMEWORKS, MODELS, DIAGRAMS

Adapted from FM 22-100, Military Leadership, October 1983, p. 49, Leadership Framework *(Page 24)*

Adapted from FM 22-100, Military Leadership, October 1983, p. 98, Ethical Reasoning Process *(Page 39)*

Adapted from FM 22-100, Military Leadership, October 1983, p. 142, Two Key Questions *(Page 62)*

Adapted from FM 22-100, Military Leadership, October 1983, p. 188, The Communication Process *(Page 77)*

Adapted from TC 25-20, A Leader's Guide to After-Action Reviews, September 1993, pps. 1-6, The AAR Process *(Page 104)*

LEADERSHIP COURSES

    I.   **Lead with Intent** – Forty (40) hour Leadership immersion course

    II.   **Decisions, Decisions, Decisions** – Four hour seminar on the formal and informal Decision Making Model©

    III.   **Managing Change** – Four hour seminar on the Human Capital Management change management methodology

    IV.   **Creating an Innovation Environment** – Four hour seminar on how to create and sustain a perpetual innovation environment

    V.   **Performance** – Four hour seminar on the performance management methodology

ANNUAL LEADERSHIP PLAN OUTLINE

Leader Name: _____

Date: _____

Year: _____

Manager/Accountability: _____

I.   Leader Philosophy

II.   Leader Mission Statement

III.   Leader SWOT

    a. Strengths
    b. Weaknesses
    c. Opportunities
    d. Threats

IV.   Goals

    a. Strengths
        i. _____
        ii. _____
        iii. _____
    b. Weaknesses
        i. _____
        ii. _____
        iii. _____
    c. New Experience(s)
        i. _____
        ii. _____
        iii. _____
    d. Job related goals
        i. _____
        ii. _____
        iii. _____

V.   Outcomes

    a. 1st Quarter
    b. 2nd Quarter
    c. 3rd Quarter
    d. 4th Quarter

VI.   Manager/Accountability Assessment